Launch that Book

Tammy Karasek

Endorsements

Launch That Book provides a step-by-step proven method of launching your book into readers' hands. A must-read for every writer who dreams of success. Tammy Karasek has taken her expertise to a new level by instructing authors how to expertly launch their books into the hands of readers.

DiAnn Mills – Canyon of Deceit – Tyndale
diannmills.com

When I was asked if I would endorse Tammy's book launch book, I couldn't agree fast enough. I've hired Tammy to launch many of my books and I can't say enough good things about her and her process to get the books into the hands of readers and onto the best-seller lists. This little guide will allow you to do the same. I honestly can't believe she's willing to share her secrets, but they're here and I encourage you to follow it. What a phenomenal tool this is for so many authors.

Run to get this book and then do what it says. You won't be sorry!

Lynette Eason, best-selling, award-winning author of the Lake City Heros series.

I know Tammy's expertise as a launch expert firsthand. Together we worked on the launch of my *Book Proposals That Sell*. A skilled professional with great experience, I'm eager for every author to read *Launch That Book!* and highly recommend it. Over 4,500 new books are published every day. You need *Launch That Book!* from Tammy Karasek to get detailed help. You will gain Tammy's insights from being on hundreds of book launches combined with the details of a creative way for you to launch your book. Mark up this book and use it over and over with each book launch.

W. Terry Whalin, bestselling author of more than 60 books.

With *Launch That Book,* author Tammy Karasek has given authors a gift beyond price. Her skill with words and sense of humor not only makes this a valuable book, but one that's fun to read. She shares her proven methodology and makes the daunting prospect of launching a book understandable. This is a book I'll bring to every writing event I attend, and I will recommend this resource to writers for year to come.

Edie Melson, author, speaker, and director of Blue Ridge Mountains Christian Writers Conference

Launch that Book

Copyright © 2025 Tammy Karasek

Revised Edition

All rights reserved.

Second Edition Published by Tammy Karasek, LLC

tammy@tammykarasek.com

ISBN 979-8-9934468-0-6

First Edition has been revised, refreshed and updated. The author retains full rights to the original work of this book. This book was originally published by Bold Vision Books under ISBN9781962705028,

Published and printed in the United States of America.

 Formatted with Vellum

Foreword

Long before I ever attempted to write a book of my own, I had a rather fanciful notion of what the process entailed. In one scenario I imagined the writer in a cabin, logs crackling in the fireplace, a steaming mug of coffee, maybe some pastries, and a gentle snowfall to complete the ambiance. In such a setting, the author generated words with ease and delight. When the story was complete, they sent it to their publisher, and while the publisher handled turning their words into a book with a cover and pages, the author immediately began writing the next book. When the publisher was finished with the book, the author would take a break from writing to go on a book tour—planned and paid in full by the publisher, of course—where they would sign the books and take photos with crowds of readers.

What can I say? I have an imagination! It's part of the job. Sure, I knew it was more work than all that, but I had no clue how wrong I was. Oh, it didn't take me long at all to realize that the days of writing in a cozy cabin would be few and far between, or that there would be months of editing and revisions that followed the completion of a story.

But never in my wildest nightmares could I have envisioned the scenario that unfolded with the publication of my first trade-length novel. Nothing prepared me for the chaos in my mind as I attempted to market my novel while simultaneously working on revisions for the second novel in the series *and* writing the third book in the series.

It was during those intense months that I fully appreciated just how much is required of authors, far beyond crafting engaging stories with unforgettable characters and breath-stealing plot twists.

And that was when I so wish I'd had access to the book you now hold in your hands.

I knew I needed help to get the word out, but I was flying blind. I gathered readers to my team, but with no real method or criteria. Once I had the team, it took hours of research on my part to even have a clue what to ask them to do. I fumbled along in that fashion for three books. Never knowing if any of it was really making a difference, being absolutely certain there was a better way, and wishing I had a plan instead of winging it.

This book would have been a lifesaver. Tammy has laid it all out for you. Step by step. From how to find the right readers for your team, to how to interact, and when to say goodbye. If you follow what she's provided for you here, this book can be your guide to a successful book launch.

I know her methods work, because after fumbling my way through the process with my first series, I was in a position to hire Tammy to run my launches for the next series. With Tammy at the helm, my books have made their way to best seller lists, my launch teams have been filled with some of the most delightful and passionate readers I've ever had the privilege of knowing, and my stress levels (at least when it comes to this aspect of the process) have hit new lows.

In an ideal world, authors would be responsible for nothing more than writing compelling stories. In the real world, authors, both independent and traditional, are ultimately responsible for every aspect of the publishing process. And all authors are expected to market their books and do whatever they can to get their books in the hands of readers.

It feels like a lot. And it is. But following Tammy's instructions will ultimately save you time and energy that you can then use to write more stories that will capture the hearts and minds of new readers.

So relax. You're in good hands. Tammy's a pro. She'll help you launch your book into the world and keep your sanity while you do it!

Lynn H. Blackburn, award-winning, best-selling author. Author of the Dive Team Investigations Series, Defend and Protect Series, and Gossamer Falls Series.

Introduction

I'm proud of you and excited for you. Why? You've purchased this book which I believe will become a resource for you to return to many times. Before I dig into the ideas and tips to use on your book launch, I want to introduce myself. Also, to explain why I'm confident to share this information with you.

With several decades of administrative experience paired with more than a decade of launch team participation in various ways, I love to talk about all the details of a launch. I not only manage launch teams for authors, I teach authors how to manage their own launch teams. I've taught about launches at the Blue Ridge Mountains Christian Writers Conference, ACFW National Conference, Carolina Christian Writers Conference as well as various ACFW local chapters throughout the US.

Since 2012, I've participated in more than 400 launch teams as of the printing of this book. I've served large publishing companies for their launches as well as individual authors still today.

From the knowledge and experience I've gained, author friends asked me for help with their teams more than six years ago. Thus, The Launch Team Geek business was created.

From my experience, I've learned a lot about an effective launch. I've experienced some phenomenal teams over the years and some, well … let's say they were less than stellar. From my participation in and assistance to authors for their launches, I've landed on a sweet spot of what works and what doesn't for my teams. This method works for me and how I manage these teams.

I'm aware launch teams are managed in various ways. I've been told others manage teams different than I do. We manage launch teams with different approaches with the same goal in mind—a great launch for the author.

I manage authors' teams myself, but I've enjoyed the option to coach those brave enough to launch on their own. And an exciting new opportunity for my launch management is the addition to work directly with a couple of large publishers and their marketing departments.

In this book, I provide the tools to equip you to do your own launch. No need to stress. I give you everything you need from start to finish to get the job done—from gathering a team, sharing graphics, to fun on launch day and more. With this book on your bookshelf, you have it at your fingertips with each book launch you do.

My system works. In fact, two of my launches were on the same day. They ended up number one and number two on the Parable Marketing Booksellers top sellers for that week. Another launch I managed, the author earned number one in two Parable categories and number three in another category. A big part of the successes was the team. My system educated, equipped and encouraged them to stay energized and eager to share the book anywhere and everywhere.

My hope for you is you'll read this book slow in order to digest each step. May you highlight, write notes in margins, dog-ear pages and return to the book often. I hope you'll need the book many times in your writing career.

Let's get to it.

Contents

*This book is dedicated to my
biggest cheerleader and best friend,
my husband, Larry Karasek.
You were there for the first edition -
and now here again for the second edition!
Thank you! Love you! Mean it!*

Chapter 1

Street Teams and Launch Teams

STREET TEAMS AND LAUNCH TEAMS—AREN'T they the same? Yes, and no. Often people use the titles and perceive them as the same thing. However, I believe they are two different teams and I see the benefit of using them as two separate teams. Bear with me as I explain why I feel this way.

Street team is a marketing term for assembling a team of people who will work apart from the office or "on the streets" in the promotion of a specific product or upcoming event. Street Team is not a new idea. Record companies have used these teams to promote new musicians and their albums for many years. Often, the record companies would gather fans of the singer or singing groups, and these fans passed out fliers, stickers or other marketing items to advertise the name of the album and the date of its release. These street team members may also call radio stations and request the new song played for more attention to it. They are, as the name states, the team on the street—A Street Team.

For authors, these same groups of people can also be called street teams. Or another term authors may use is reader groups. These street teams or reader groups are fan clubs for an artist or creative who seeks help in getting the word out about an upcoming release of their newest project. Whether the item is a book, album or other product, these fans will spread the word about the item for the artist.

Street teams are people who love the creative or artist and are his or her biggest fans. Fans will follow the author and the books the author writes throughout their writing career. They will continue to talk about the books and the author to other readers long after book launch conversations expire. Street Teams will often share information about the author's books on their own social media if or when the author shares graphics in their street team's private Facebook group. A private Facebook street team group allows you to build your readership, share your book updates, and also to advertise your newsletter sign-ups. All a great resource to build the author's platform. This activity happens throughout the year, not only at a launch time.

For the launch teams I manage, a launch team is a team of 35-50 fans of the author selected to share about a book's upcoming release. As of this writing, the private Facebook group is still a viable place to gather the team and share graphics for them to share. Some people use email only for this, but I've had more problems with folks not being able to download the graphics and share from an email. Make sure you instruct the team on how to download the graphics and use on their social media sites. It's imperative to educate and equip your team for them to be able to help promote your book. For instance, Facebook doesn't allow anyone to share from a private group so make sure to explain that to your team and how to download the graphic and share from their computer. They are doing you a favor by sharing your info, do them the favor of making it possible and easy to share the graphics and information.

Others use Discord to gather the team to talk about all things launch for that book. In my experience so far, many of the people on the teams I manage are not interested in signing up for another social media site. And if they sign up for this app so they can be on the team, their influence will be low as they're new to the site and may not have many followers there yet. I'm not sold on it as an efficient use for a launch team's efforts at this point. However, if that is where you regularly engage with your readers, then that would make sense to work through that app.

In the private launch group on Facebook, members can share the graphics provided, as well as other tasks the author may ask the team to do. Some folks may come from within the street team, but not necessarily. I will explain in a future chapter my method of choosing a team. For now, I want you to understand my thoughts between the two types of teams and how you can best utilize their value. Once you know the benefits and function of each, you can better equip each team.

Am I right and others are wrong? Not at all. This is how I understand the best use of fans of the authors to get outstanding success in launching a book and I've seen good results. Other authors who launch their own books or other launch team managers may use a different strategy for one or the other or both. Some choose to only use a street team group, but I believe the logistics of who will share, if you want to give any gifts at the end of a launch, or how you will keep track may become convoluted. I see the benefit of utilizing both teams for a better return on your invested time.

That's not to say you can't use only a street team and ask them to share graphics, complete specific tasks and leave reviews for the book if your street team is small. However, back to the logistics of giving everyone within your Facebook street team group—if it's large—a paperback book could be costly if you're the one mailing the books and if you're traditionally published, most large publishers won't provide over fifty books. I am unaware of any small publishers who mail any number of paperback books to a team. Now some of the larger publishers are moving towards NetGalley or BookFunnel digital copies for team members. The other point to consider, even if you're going to send the street team a PDF, you're losing out on sales when going over the fifty-member mark.

The goal for a street team is to grow that particular

group as large as you can. Yes, you may absolutely use them to share graphics and talk about your new book release if they are willing. A few here and there throughout the launch session are great. But you don't want to burn them out asking for a favor often to help promote your books. A couple a month wouldn't hurt. Every day or week throughout the month? Don't do it. Much better to keep the street team in the game and continue to grow your fan base. Then let the short-term launch team help for that specific session to assist you in the launch of your newest book.

Chapter 2

I Only Need a Launch Team If I Independently Publish, Right?

IF ONLY I could say yes to that question. Truth is, whether you will publish as an Independent, Hybrid, or Traditional author, I recommend you have a launch team. Whether you hire a launch team manager or run the team on your own is a matter of choice. Either will work.

People often tell me they could never manage a launch team. I agree some people's schedules may already be overloaded or they fear they don't have the knowledge to run a team on their own. Yet with the right tools and training, I believe most people can lead a successful launch team and enjoy a stress-free experience. My goal is to educate and equip you with the tools to run your own launch team should you choose to do so.

I would fib if I said there's nothing to the management of a team. A lot of work needs done. Then again, the book you've written took a great deal of work and effort as well. Don't stop the effort and momentum you've started once you type *The End*. I've heard many authors say writing the book was the simple part.

Now the marketing and all the next steps to get the book into the readers' hands are the hard parts. The launch team is one item of your marketing plan and an integral part of the success in sales for your book. Publishers won't do the launch of your book. That will be your responsibility, no matter which way you choose to publish. That's not to say they won't give you some extra help. Don't count on much, though.

In my experience, a traditional, large publisher may offer you some help in a launch by creating graphics of your cover and submitting your book to retailers and online retail sites, or some postcards and bookmarks. They may also offer help with promoting your book in their company's quarterly catalogs, on their social media accounts, or they might even offer a giveaway contest on Goodreads. They used to provide you with paperback ARCs (advanced reader copies) sent to your launch team of fifty or less members—but most have moved to a link to NetGalley or Book Funnel for the teammates to download as I said before. They will not assist you in selecting a team, provide more graphics, or handle the management of a team. That is your responsibility.

A traditional small publisher does not do as much of the above-mentioned items. They often are short-staffed and cannot help much with products for the launch of your book. I've seen small publishers some-times provide a couple of graphics or a post card and bookmark pdf for the author to present to a printer or for the author to print on card stock at home. I've not seen a small publisher provide any ARCs to an author to mail to their team members. I've only experienced a digital copy of the book presented to the author for distribution to a launch team. Often an author will share their PDF or upload their book to Book Funnel, which allows only the people who receive the link to download the book for their personal use and often the link expires within a couple of weeks so it can no longer be downloaded.

Book Funnel is a subscription-based program for authors to use. The download of a book can only be used one time for the recipient. You can use Book Funnel to deliver eBooks, reader magnets, and more. It's not an expensive program, and can be valuable for sharing your work with readers.

If you choose to Independent Publish, then you will be the one to manage all aspects of the launch of your book, unless you hire a launch team manager. You will create all graphics, postcards, or bookmarks you choose to use. You will be the person to instruct what you'd like help with from your launch team. Don't let all that is involved with a launch team deter you from having a team. It's a helpful tool in the book's release. Like I said above, with the knowledge of helpful tools and guidance, you can manage your own team.

In the chapters to come, I will discuss further what

the team can do for you in getting the message out regarding the upcoming release of your book.

While there are so many options of items you can—and should—do in the year prior to a launch session, this book focuses on the launch session. Here are some suggestions during the year prior to release day: you could secure interviews on podcasts, online or in-person TV interviews, and schedule a launch team release party and secure your location.

Join the Blue Ridge Reader Connections group which offers many benefits to authors. This is a great way to gain new followers and help you grow your platform and influence. The low-cost yearly fee is worth the marketing it allows. You can find more information on the website, blueridgereaderconnections.com

You have a number of options for you to do before the book releases, but that's for another book. Social media remains a hot topic of debate regarding book promotion. Some say social media isn't for selling books, so don't use it. I agree and disagree. The title tells you exactly what it is—it's social. It's not called selling media, or social bookselling! The best way to sell anything is by word of mouth. This gives an item or product—like your book—credibility because the person sharing about it has read the book. Many people prefer to make a purchase once they've read a review or recommendation about the product. I don't blame them.

Don't let someone's opinion of social media deter you from using what you can through your social media sites. If your thought is you will join every social media channel that is available to sell your books, this will disappoint you—in a big way. Join social media sites where you believe your audience is. Please don't join every one of the social media sites. If that's not where your readers will be, don't give yourself one more item to manage on your to-do-list.

For example, my audience is not the teen and twenty-year-old crowd, so Snapchat will not bring me a good ROI (return of investment) of my time. Facebook, like it or not, still has a lot of followers and people who are okay with using it from thirty years old and up. Though it's most popular with the fifty years old and above. Sometimes the age average of the sites ebbs and flows. Do your homework, see where most of your readership hangs out. Be aware of your genre, the general audience age for that genre, and start there.

Social media used properly in a book launch will gain you the attention you seek. Eyes on your book. Yet you alone can only mention the book to your circle of influence. That's where a launch team comes into play.

When you gather a team of fifty—my recommended number—those fifty people combined have a far greater reach than you alone will. With that in mind, I work a specific way to select a launch team to further expand the reach of talking about your book. I explain this further in Chapter Five.

A launch team, no matter how your book is published, is not the only tool you will need for the launch of your book, but it is excellent and necessary item in your book release tool belt. And I'm all about excellent tools in your tool belt.

Accept the fact you will need a launch team. So, let's move on, and I'll teach you how to create one, then manage that team.

Chapter 3

Create a Timeline for Your Launch Session

ONE OF THE best ways to stay on track and focused on the launch of your book is to set yourself up with an actionable plan. A timeline is the ticket for this. By having this in place way before the actual launch session, you can prepare some items you will use during the launch to help you stay organized and less stressed.

What I do for each of the launch teams I manage is to first look at the scheduled launch date. From that date, I count back twelve weeks. That time period becomes my launch session. This is not the exact time you will work with the team, but it is where you, the author/launch manager, will put all pieces into place so the team and launch session will run smooth.

Prior to the start of your session, you need your book cover and need to also decide how you will provide the team with a book—a PDF or form of digital copy of the book or your publisher will send paperback

ARCs. These often are not the final copy and may say uncorrected copy on the cover. If that's the case, remind your team of this, or you may receive many emails with corrections for you. How you will provide the book is an important piece that needs to be discussed with your publisher before you plan to create a team. When you create a Launch Team Application, the type of book needs to be clear on the form so they know which type of book they'll receive, either a digital or paperback copy. I recommend you type this is bold print.

Depending on how you will publish (Traditional/Hybrid/Independent), make sure if you're not going Independent, the conversation with your publisher will happen early on as to what style of book they will give you to distribute to your team. The second question you need to ask is what date will the ARC or digital copy be ready for and available to present to the team members.

If the publisher doesn't give you at least a six or seven-week window between the availability of the ARC and launch date, you need to request either the ARC comes sooner, or they push the Launch Date out on the calendar. The most successful launch provides team members with books in time to be able to at least read part, if not all, of the book before you ask them to share graphics and other tasks.

Again, when you create the Launch Team Application, you'll need to include this information of the type of book they will receive. I also highly recommend you place it in your email or newsletter as well, so it's clear to the readers when they apply. Some people prefer what type of book they will read for a launch team. It's best to be up front with the applicants, so you don't choose a team, then a few inform you they will not take part after all because they will only read paperbacks. Trust me, it happens more than you would think. I'm finding more and more team members will not work on teams that provide digital copies.Being up front saves you the frustration of having forty to fifty people apply, get started, then quit when you send them a digital copy of your book. I learned the hard way so you don't have to. Let them know.

When you've received the date the ARCs will be available and confirmed the launch date, you can create a workable timeline. This doesn't matter if you handwrite on a sheet of paper, type it in a Word document or get all fancy with a spreadsheet. The important part is what will work for you. You will refer to this often to keep you on track, so make it easy and convenient to use.

Other activity will happen around you during your launch session. One of those activities is life. You'll need something to remember where you were, and what you did last for and with the team. While you wrote your book, you saw how quick you could get derailed. All of us can relate to this, so don't skip this part. You'll be so glad you did at the end of the launch. The good part—you are now equipped for that next launch of yours.

On your timeline sheet or chart, list your launch date at the end. Looking at your calendar, count back twelve weeks. This will be the start of the launch session for you. I say twelve because you need to be mindful of your own personal schedule. You need time to create your application and time for the team to apply for a week or two. Then you need to give yourself time to sort through the names to choose a solid team. It depends on your schedule, but a couple of days should suffice to sort through the spreadsheet of names you'll receive. This could take you a couple of weeks from the date you sent the application out to the time spent to select the actual team. Make sure you allow enough time to do it. You don't want to rush through the team selection process.

After team selection, you are at about week seven from launch week. On your sheet, create a week's heading (week seven, week six, etc.) all the way to launch week, leaving space to fill in the tasks of each week. Under each heading, you will put what you want the team to do for your launch that week. Also, you'll add if this is a week you'll have a drawing or a Facebook Live which I explain in later chapters. You'll make notation of any emails you will send to the team on the proper week it will be done.

For the timeline, each week I put Tuesday and Thursday as days I ask the team to complete particular actions. You choose what days you prefer and use that as your days for your team. For now, I'll share my actual schedule.

On Tuesday, I often create a graphic that says Tuesday Task. I will take an item off of the task list (Chapter Ten) that I want to highlight, such as "If you've liked the book, would you consider purchasing a copy for a friend, your library or one of the new local neighborhood library boxes on launch day?"

On the task list I create for the team, I've listed many tasks any team member can do on their own throughout the session, but during the Tuesday Task graphic, I choose specific ones I would like them to do and I use this way to draw attention to the importance of it. The graphic has the task, but the wording on the post explains in more detail the benefit or instructions for the task.

On Thursday each week, I create a graphic for them to share. A graphic could also be one your publisher has given you, like Preorder, and later in the launch session, Available Now. Publishers don't give you many, but may give you a couple, so use them. I also make sure to have the #booktitle and the author website on every graphic to act as a watermark as well as where else someone could find more information about the author, or YOU!

Above I mentioned emails. On the timeline, I will also mark the week I want certain emails to go to the team. Such as a reminder for anyone who hasn't joined the Facebook Group yet by the end of the first week, the task list, helpful review tips, and the final task check-in and survey. This timeline helps keep me stay attuned of what needs to go and when. I usually email the review tip sheet at the end of the week when I see most team members post they've received the book, whether digital or paperback. Then they'll be prepared with the instructions on how to give a great review before they post them. There is no way to gauge how fast the team members will read the book.

Also in this timeline, I will note what week I will have drawings if any will be done. Next chapter, I will get into drawings and gifts in more detail. For this chapter, I'm talking about the need to chart out when (or if) those will be done, so you don't get to the end of the launch session and realize you forgot to do them. Tip for this, if you state you will have drawings and fun in the session without giving away when those will happen, you can save yourself the embarrassment if you forgot a drawing. You can move it forward a week or lump it with the end of launch drawing. Don't sweat it. Remember, the timeline is for you and your eyes only, but it helps you keep on track.

This timeline is helpful to achieve that smooth launch session we all want. No need to stress if you shared a specific graphic or not. You've already decided when you want it to be posted. And definitely take advantage of the option to schedule those posts within the Facebook Group. Life happens and you'll be less stressed to keep the team humming along fine while you handle those issues because you scheduled posts ahead of time.

An example of a timeline:

. . .

WEEK ONE OF LAUNCH TEAM SESSION

(Seven weeks before Launch)

*Note: Whatever graphic you make the entire launch session, be sure to put your book's hashtag and your website on the bottom in small but readable letters.

MONDAY:

Team email–Congratulations you've made the Launch Team

In this email, link to Closed Launch Team Facebook Group to join

Welcome graphic in Facebook group, welcome post and a couple of questions to introduce themselves. Leave the group as visible until all members are in.

TUESDAY:

Post the screenshot of the notifications with it marked All Posts.

Instruct members to do the same so they don't miss info and graphics provided.

THURSDAY:

Let the team share their first graphic you provide in the Facebook Group that says: "Coming Soon." Explain they'll need to download the graphic and share to their own social media sites since we can't share from Groups.

Inform them wherever they share anything about the book to use the hashtag of your book title, genre and your website in their post. This allows you to put the hashtag into a search bar and find out where the team shared your book info.

WEEK TWO OF LAUNCH TEAM SESSION
(Six weeks before Launch)

TUESDAY:

Post your first Tuesday Task to mark their account on Goodreads and BookBub that they're reading your book.

*Note: I create a graphic that says Tuesday Task, then change the task written each week using the same graphic background.

THURSDAY:

Email the Task Checklist you already created, so the team has it to work from. Explain in the email you will remind them about some, but if they'd like to do any of the tasks ahead of time (except the Amazon review), they can do that.

Post in the FB group to check their emails for a

helpful tool (The Task List) for ideas to share the news about the book.

FRIDAY:

If you have the digital copy, email a copy or book link to each launch team member. Unfortunately, If you are traditionally published, you don't have control over this.

WEEK THREE OF LAUNCH TEAM SESSION

(Five weeks before Launch)

MONDAY:

If you have a drawing, create a graphic that says: "Drawing this Friday." In the text above the graphic, tell the team to post in the thread below, the items they've done off the Task List and their name will go in the drawing for each item they list. If you'll announce the winner in a Facebook Live, include that in the message or on the graphic so they can mark their calendars to join you if they can. Also, give them the time and time zone.

TUESDAY:

Share the Pre-order graphic, whether the publisher provided one or you create your own.

THURSDAY:

Post the Graphic for the Goodreads giveaway for the team to share if your publisher provided one. If you are an Independent published author, you can also do a Goodreads giveaway. It's about $130 per book giveaway and the time of this printing. If you are not, create a graphic of your book on a chair, someone reading it or something fun—get creative. Post in the FB group for the team to share.

Draw a name from those that submitted tasks they've done in the thread below your drawing announcement on Monday of this week. You can use a raffle app to do in a live Facebook post on Friday, or the old-fashioned way of names on slips of paper and draw one. Your choice.

FRIDAY:

If you did a drawing, post a graphic that says: "Winner" and insert the name on the graphic you created before you post.

Do a Facebook Live if you choose and announce the winner, then leave the recorded message up so all can see it. Also, you can leave more for them in the message if you want.

Send the prize to the winner.

. . .

WEEK FOUR OF LAUNCH TEAM SESSION

(Four weeks before Launch)

TUESDAY:

Tuesday Task–Suggest the team share about your book in their book club or other Facebook groups where they are permitted to share.

THURSDAY:

First Line graphic to share. Take the first line of your book and create a graphic with that line on the graphic. Try to find photos that coordinate with your book/story. Then post in the FB group for the team to share.

WEEK FIVE OF LAUNCH TEAM SESSION

(Three weeks before Launch)

MONDAY:

Email to team the Helpful Tips for reviews sheet you have already prepared.

Graphic to team in FB group to check emails for review tips sheet.

If you will do a drawing this week, use a graphic you've created that says: "Drawing this Friday".

TUESDAY:

Tuesday Task—If you liked the book, would you consider buying a book on launch day and gift it to a friend, donate it to your church library, a nursing home or one of the neighborhood library boxes?

THURSDAY:

Create a graphic and post in the FB group for the team to share.

Draw a name from those who submitted tasks they've done if you're doing a drawing to announce tomorrow.

FRIDAY:

If you did a drawing, post a graphic that says: "Winner" and insert the name on the graphic before you post.

Do a Facebook Live if you choose, and announce the winner. Leave the recorded message up so all can see when they can. You can leave more for them in the message.

Send the prize to the winner.

. . .

WEEK SIX OF LAUNCH TEAM SESSION
(Two weeks before Launch)

TUESDAY:
Tuesday Task—"Many of you have finished the book. Now's a great time to leave those reviews on the sites that will accept them (not Amazon). Remember, write the review once, then copy and paste to other sites.

THURSDAY:
Create a graphic and post in the FB group for the team to share.

WEEK SEVEN OF LAUNCH TEAM SESSION
(One week before Launch)

MONDAY:
If you have a drawing, share the graphic that says: "Drawing this Friday".

TUESDAY:
Tuesday Task—Suggest a mini review of the book on Facebook or Instagram.

Have the team put your book's hashtag into the search bar on their social media sites, go to those listed and love them, and ask them to leave a comment on some to keep the graphics rolling on the newsfeeds.

THURSDAY:

Share a graphic for the team to share, like a pre-order graphic for their social media sites.

Draw a name from those who submitted tasks they've done if you're doing a drawing to announce tomorrow.

FRIDAY:

If you did a drawing, post a graphic that says: "Winner" and insert the name on the graphic before you post.

Do a Facebook Live, if you choose and announce the winner. Then leave the recorded message up so all can see it. You can leave more for them in the message, such as a thank you for their efforts, reminder about the reviews so they are ready for Amazon on launch day next week, etc.

Send the prize to the winner.

WEEK EIGHT OF LAUNCH TEAM SESSION
LAUNCH WEEK!!!

. . .

MONDAY:

Reminder to write their reviews today if they haven't, so they can copy and paste their <u>honest review</u> for Amazon or be ready to copy and paste if they've already done the other sites. Remind them to refer to the Helpful Tips for Reviews sheets and don't forget the Disclaimer at the bottom of *all* reviews. Also a reminder to share on their social sites at least three times this week.

TUESDAY–LAUNCH DAY! (If your launch day is Tuesday. Most I've managed are, so I put that here. Your launch day may be different.)

Make a graphic and post to remind the team "Get those honest Amazon reviews up today!" And as early as possible. Amazon will check on them, so we need them to have the time to do that. We <u>*want*</u> as much traction on Launch Day so the numbers in the various categories rise for the book.

Now that the book is available, make sure you add the buy links to the book seller sites your book is listed for sale. This helps shoppers go right to the "shelf" to purchase the book. Once click shopping.

*Note: Consider splitting the team in two and have half post on Amazon on launch day and half the next day if you have a full team of fifty. From time to time, Amazon changes how many reviews they will allow on the actual launch day. Other times, no problem. We never know how they will run, we do the best we can.

Provide a Launch Day Graphic for them to share that says Now Available.

WEDNESDAY:

If you plan to send a Final Task Check-in List Survey, today is the day to email that to the team. (I explain this in Chapter 18.)

THURSDAY:

Graphic created that says Now Available for team to share. Do this early in the day.

Make sure you add the buy links to the book seller sites your book is listed for sale.

A post with or without a graphic to reminder team to get those reviews in, it's not too late. A couple of hours after Now Available post.

FRIDAY:

Post for the Team: Look over your Task Checklist. Are there still items not done? Is there something you could still do for the launch? Go do those now if possible.

Post to inform team of the Final FB Live to announce the Grand Prize winner if you will have one next Friday. This is to remind them to complete and submit the Launch Team Survey if you sent them to the team before next Thursday night.

WEEK AFTER LAUNCH—FINISH UP WEEK:

MONDAY:

Create and post a graphic of your book letting readers know it's available. Don't forget the buy links to the book seller sites your book is listed for sale.

Create another Reminder of FB Live for Grand Prize and Farewell if you are doing either of these. Tell them time and time zone.

TUESDAY:

Another push for reviews and other shares of graphics they may not have shared yet.

FRIDAY:

Create and post a graphic early in the morning of your book letting readers know it's available. Don't forget those the buy links to the book seller sites your book is listed for sale.

Final Facebook Live and final drawing, again if you've chosen to do this.

Last request for honest reviews on Amazon and

any other sites you know your book has been uploaded to.

Create a graphic that says Thanks for all you've done etc. and the announcement for the winner of the final drawing if you're doing a grand prize drawing.

If you are not doing a final drawing, this is the day to email the team (or a handwritten note even better) with a thank you and let them know this concludes the launch session.

Final graphic that says Thank You. Also in the text to accompany this graphic, let the team know that the launch of your book is complete.

The timeline example I've included in this chapter is provided as a general overview of the one I use. Feel free to add more to your timeline to help you stay on track. Create the timeline, then let it work for you. A dedicated launch timeline is a wonderful tool to keep the stress low because you will know what you need to do next. I suggest you read it a few weeks ahead and prepare the items you will need early.

Chapter 4

To SWAG or Not to SWAG

I'M SURE BY NOW, we've all heard the word SWAG thrown around. I'm also sure we have an idea of what the word means. A couple years ago, I learned that SWAG is an acronym for Stuff We All Get. I thought it was funny, but it made sense.

Authors often give a gift to thank their team for the assistance. Some people love all the gifts they receive from authors, whether they've received the item after a purchase of the book or for a gift after participating on a launch team. Still others don't care if they receive any type of gift. You'll never know who on your team will appreciate a gift. Decide what you'd like to give, if anything, and go with it.

There's quite a collection of assorted gifts in my office from being on all these teams. I guess I'm a collector of my SWAG, because I have it all in one box. I tell myself to get the items out and use and enjoy them. Yet, I don't want to use them up. I know. I'm a weird one. My box sits in my office filled with all the cool SWAG I've received over these last fourteen years of launch teams. Well, except for the two chocolate bars from an author who sends her launch team a chocolate bar wrapped with her book cover artwork. So cute. They always arrived melted. But I live with a chocoholic, so he put the chocolate in the freezer so it could firm up again and be enjoyed once solid. As I tell you this, picture my head shaking and my eyes in a roll. That guy learned to recognize the familiar color-padded envelopes every time one arrived from this author and would open them to retrieve those bars of chocolate. How rude. Just kidding, I didn't mind. It's more fun to poke fun at his ability to see the brightly-colored envelope and know what was inside without opening it.

So, what kind of SWAG is out there, you might ask? I've received:

Neck scarves with the author's branding, or another with only books

Pencils with my name and the book's name on it

Bracelets of all kinds

Hand-made bookmarks with charms

Ecard gifts to Amazon, Barnes & Noble, Starbucks, etc.

Mini flashlights

Flash drive with their logo

Game pieces to the game that correspond to their story world

Those chocolate bars I mentioned with the book cover (Don't recommend these!)

Small recipe book

Handmade fabric purses

Book sleeves

Necklaces

Tote bags

Small engraved wooden cutting boards

Engraved wooden spoons

Embroidered towels with a line from their story

Stickers with a one liner from their story

Autographed copies of the book

Notecards with artwork significant to the story

Bookmarks made by the publisher

Handwritten thank-you notes

Still, other launch teams did not send gifts or SWAG at all. On some teams, you earned a charm or pin when you completed a task. Others ran it more like a competition—with each task you did that week, your name earned another entry. Still, other teams weren't a competition, but you earned points toward a gift tier that was in place and the team knew what they would receive at certain levels.

When operating your own launch team, you may do any of the above. Or none of it. You may have another idea altogether. To have any type of SWAG or gifts for your launch is up to you. Though you need to remember if you've promised something like drawings with prizes, make sure you can do those and can send them out promptly, for your sake and those awaiting the prize.

Most of the SWAG ideas will cost money to purchase. The exception will be if you go the route of a traditional publisher, which may provide you with postcards or bookmarks. But you will still need to pay for postage. While you might like to send something to a winner or the winners, remember that is double expense. First to buy the gift and second to mail it. Be mindful of the budget you set for this and stay within that financial parameter you've given.

Some authors have chosen gifts from Amazon for a couple of drawings and or a Grand Prize. After the selection of the winner for the drawing, the author went to Amazon, ordered a reader's gift, and had it sent directly to the Grand Prize winner. Items like book socks, book clip-on light, blanket with books on it, any reader and/or book themed gifts. Once selected, they had gifts shipped straight to the home of the winner instead of buying something before the launch, wait until they announced the winner, and then take the time and pay the cost of shipping it to the team member from their local post office.

If you're already mailing them a paperback book, or your publisher is, it's fine to send them a paper bookmark and a handwritten note at the end of the launch. Although, if you love giving gifts or showing gratitude through gifts, you can do that.

I'm a gift-giver, so I would lean toward a gift myself. But I've had authors who gave nothing. I'm fine with that, too. I received their book to read and have the gift of a paperback or PDF book in my hands, and I'm grateful for that.

The best advice I can give you is to stay within your budget—both financial and time-wise—and you'll be fine.

Chapter 5

Create Graphics to Use for Your Launch Session

WE HAVE several programs and applications to choose from to use to create these graphics. My personal favorite is Canva. But we also have PicMonkey, Adobe, Book Brush (designed for authors), and Pablo. Besides Canva, I've used PicMonkey and Book Brush. I use the paid version of Canva and Book Brush because of the versatility and features that are offered. I like them because they consistently add new features and I find them user friendly, although both take a bit for you to feel comfortable and explore all the options they offer. Definitely get in there and play.

But whatever you find best for you to work with should be the program you use. I know some folks use a mix of PicMonkey, Canva and Book Brush for the different nuances that each have and blend them to achieve the graphic they want. Personally, I use Book Brush to make fast 3-D versions of the book, then download and upload back into Canva for creating my graphics.

During the first week of the session, you will create a Facebook group header, provided you have the book cover already. You'll need to upload the cover of your book into Canva (or app you're using) if you haven't already, to be used in the headers and the other graphics for the launch.

To make this header, I use Canva to do the header and the graphics to come. Then all my graphics and book cover photos are all in one spot for quick use. With the above sites, you can save whatever you make, and you have free use of the photographs they have on their site. Be careful of photography sites should you choose to look for other photos for your graphics. Some say they are royalty free but may not be. Save yourself a lawsuit and do your homework on the site you'd like to use. Take the extra time and research the site, going off their site to read reviews or commentaries about the site as well.

While creating the Facebook header, you'll also want to create the header you will use for your Launch Team Application to be used in Google Forms. Because the sizes often change in these applications, search for current sizes for them through Google or your favorite search engine. When those answers come up, check the date of the post. Trust me on this. Learn from my experience. A suggested search would be: current size for Facebook header. Make sure it's a recent post on the sizes.

To make the headers, go to Canva (or your preferred graphic creator) to create a design with custom dimensions. As of this printing of the book, a Facebook Header size is 1800 x 640 px and a Google Form size is 1800 x 475 px (the aspect ratio is 4:1 or four times wider than tall). But please double check the current size, or create with the sizes above and see how it fits when you create the item. Adjust if you need to.

In Canva, go to the button on the homepage that says Create a Design and click it for the drop-down menu. Go to the bottom and choose Custom Size. In the boxes, you will put the size you want. For a Facebook Header, start with 1800 x 640 px. Once you've chosen the size, you will be taken to the creator page with that particular size showing. With this, you can add your book cover you've uploaded, the wording you want and the background you will choose from the backgrounds on the left-hand side list of options, or photos if you want a photo from the same left-side list. You can adjust colors and move the items around until you're happy with what you've created. Then I suggest you save the graphics in a new folder with your current book title for ease of finding them quick.

No matter what graphic or header you are creating, once you've brought your book over to the project but before you cover over your book with options, click on the book while it's on the graphic, go up to the top toolbar and click on the word Position. You'll want to click Position, then a large drop down will appear to the left of your work area. You will want to choose forward so the book doesn't get buried with words or other details you might add. This will allow your book to stay on top of the background or photo where you want it. Now you can click back onto the background you've chosen and complete the stretch to fit the entire space of the background on the project.

Save the design you've created. Make sure you name the design so you can find it. You'll do this by going to the upper left on the top bar. Click on File for the drop-down menu. On the top line, you'll click on the pencil to edit the name of the graphic with something like – Launch Facebook Header and date. Whatever will set that apart from other Launch Headers you'll make for future books. Then scroll down and save.

On the upper right, download this header to your computer by clicking on the Share button so it's ready for you to build the Facebook Group, which I'll explain in Chapter Five.

If you have the paid version of Canva, you can make a copy of this graphic and resize it quick. If you don't have the paid plan, you will need to do the above process again from scratch for the Launch Team Application Header. When you do the resize in the paid plan, you will need to adjust where the book sits and the size of it. Also, the wording you have will need to be changed to say application and the sizing will need changed too. These are easy to do once you get in there and play. Don't be afraid to change things around and switch colors and add elements. Have fun with it. Canva is a lot of fun to create with.

While you're in the app you're using to create your Facebook header, make the Launch Team Application Header as well. When you've chosen your project and created the size, drag your book cover over to the project.

After you've chosen the background, you like that will complement your book cover, you'll want to add text to that graphic. Using hour personal information, I suggest:

Name of Your Book
By – Your Name
Launch Team Application
Launch Date: Actual Date Book Releases
Please submit by midnight (insert date) and Time Zone

This submission deadline date should be approximately ten weeks out from launch day. Please be mindful of your schedule, too. You'll want to give them about one to one and a half weeks to apply and then a few days after that for you to sort through the applicants to find the team. Following this schedule, you should be able to send the Welcome to the Team email with the Facebook Group Link to the team about eight weeks ahead of the launch date. You won't have them work those entire eight weeks, but this allows time for everyone to receive the emails, come over to the Facebook Group and get cozy in their new hangout for the next few weeks.

Now, let's talk about those graphics you'll create for the team. You will do the same step as above by going to Create a Design, choose Custom Size and put in 1350 x 1080 px. This will give you the correct size for posts on Facebook. Be aware these can sometimes change sizes to fit, adjust if or when needed. I can't explain it, but what is cool, this size also fits for Instagram and X. But be aware, always check these details from time to time. Facebook often changes those sizes.

In making the graphic, I'll say it again, have fun. You've chosen the graphic size and you're on the creator page, next, pull your book cover over to the blank white square that you have uploaded into Canva already. By pulling the book cover over first, you can now select backgrounds and see if they match, coordinate, or compete with your book cover. You want the book to stand out on the background, no matter if you've chosen a solid color, a photo they have within the program or even a photo you've uploaded yourself. Complement is good, blend in is not.

Sometimes you can move around the book to make it stand out better on the other side, raise or lower it, or place an element behind it to frame it. In the elements file, you can grab a shape, like a rectangle and place it behind the book. To get it behind, you will go to the bar across the top, click on Position, and bring the item you have your cursor on (either book or element) and click on either forward or backward, whichever you need.

Now you've created a graphic with the book cover and chosen a background you like, you can create the other graphics you will ask the launch team to share. You should create eight to ten minimum graphics for the team to use throughout the launch period. If you are a traditional published author, graphics are items they may provide for you. Sometimes, small publishers will provide a couple, but not usually. You may have to ask for them.

The graphics I'm used to receiving are a Preorder, Goodreads Giveaway, Available Now, Blank with the cover of the book on a coordinating background and sometimes a few with that same background and lines from the book. Your method of publishing will determine if you will receive pre-made graphics or not. However, as easy as they are to make in Canva, it's good to make several specific graphics as soon as you have a book cover to use.

Those graphics are Welcome to the Team, Preorder, Available Now, and several with book quotes. Use the book cover and complementary colors of the cover and enjoy the process. Often, once you create the graphics, more ideas will come to you, so create more for the team to share, but not too many. Give them one at a time, no need to give them multiples at a time. Plus this takes extra time for you to create them all. I've had team members say they are overwhelmed getting four or five to choose from each week or twice a week. Also, on my Task Check List form, I suggest the team members create a graphic to share. I've now added that idea to one of the Tuesday Tasks to remind them of this.

The creativity of some members has blown me away. A couple folks have made some gorgeous graphics. Once they've made and posted the graphics, I jump in there and challenge the team to use as many of the graphics the others have made as they can. It often gets the others enticed to join in on the fun.

A suggestion would be to run a contest for only that week and do it early in the launch session. Everyone who would like to do it, make a graphic and share in the group by Thursday at, say, 8:00 p.m. Then create a poll on Friday morning and let the team vote on the favorite for the week. You can do this right in the group.

You can present the winner with a $10 ecard for whatever company you choose. Then do another one about two weeks out from launch day with another small prize. Let the team know those graphics are free to be shared on their social media sites. Tell them to download the graphics and share away. And always use the book's hashtag. Then challenge everyone to put the hashtag in the search bar, go find as many of them as they can, then give them a love click instead of the thumbs up. Even better, leave a comment too.

Remind them to use only graphics made with royalty free photos to avoid issues where they're not needed. Nobody wants to be sued for using a photo that doesn't belong to them, for sure not the author when the author's name is on a graphic they didn't create. Team members, once instructed on this, understand and are good about where they get those photos. Be careful. Some photo sites say they are free and available for use. But there have been lawsuits where other folks have uploaded photos they thought were great to share without having permission to share to the site. Good intention or not, the photo wasn't their personal photo to share.

Chapter 6

Create a Facebook Group

ONCE YOU'VE SENT out your Launch Team Application, it's time to create the Facebook Group. Authors use different ways to communicate with their teams, such as email only, texting, or other computer applications like Discord, Slack, or Telegram to name some. But I have found that most team members still use Facebook, and for what I use it for on the launch team, it serves its purpose well. When I've checked into several of the options out there, I found that more than 70 percent of my team members didn't want to sign up for a new social network and learn it for an eight-week session. And when it comes down to it, they will not have many followers to share about your book on their brand-new platform they've recently signed up for

My experience with Facebook Groups has presented significant results, for now I will continue to use them until my results prove differently. I want to make sure the teams I've chosen can work without stress. I want them to stick with the launch session. You must decide where your team will work from and what best works for you as well. For this book, I'll be talking about Facebook Groups, but many of the items I'll speak about will work with the other sites also.

Another option can be to use your Google Drive to upload graphics and information you wish to share with your team, then share that file with them through an email with the link to your Google file.

For the purpose of this book, I will explain the use of the Facebook group to work with your launch team.

You've already created the header for Facebook in the last chapter when you also made the application header. If not, you'll need to go back and make one now. And if you've downloaded the header from the app you used, you can upload this header into the Facebook Group you will make next.

Once you have your header, sign into your Facebook profile. We're going to create a new Facebook Group. If you've not made one before, follow the next steps:

1. Go to your home page on Facebook. On the left side, scroll down until you see the icon that says Groups. Click on that.
2. It will now bring a menu that says Groups. Scroll down a bit to a blue box that says +Create new group and click on that.

3. This will bring up the place where you will create your Facebook Group. It will blink in the group name box. I recommend you don't name the group with "Your Book Title Launch Team." Rather do something that seems somewhat vague. The key is that it can't be found as a launch team should someone be looking for those who aren't on the team. For myself I might use my first name and hangout like, Tammy's Book Readers Hangout. Or Tammy's Readers. This group will go away in eight weeks anyway, unless you name it with a plan to turn it into a street team, private group after this launch.

4. Next box you will choose is Privacy. As you work to create the group, make sure you create it as a private group and hidden. You don't want it to be found as you create and put in the elements you will use. Scroll down now and click on the bright blue box which says create. You now have a Facebook group for your launch.

5. Later, once you've chosen a team and are ready to send them the welcome letter with the link to the Facebook Group, you will go to Group Settings and mark the group as visible instead of hidden so the team can ask to join with the link you will send them in their welcome letter. Also move down

that drop-down menu to Manage Membership and change the setting for who can approve member requests. Otherwise, everyone will receive the notification to approve a new member or will let others know where to join the group. Once the team has all joined the private launch team group, go back to Group Settings and return the group back to hidden. This keeps others from finding the group and asking to join throughout the session.

6. Now you will go to the top of the page where a photo is. This step is like when you added a photo on your personal profile. A refresher: on the far-right bottom of the photo is a box that says edit. This is how you will upload the Facebook header you already made. When you click edit, a new menu will come up. You want to choose upload photo.

7. If you have already downloaded your Facebook header, you will be able to grab the header and then click upload. It will take a couple seconds for that to happen.

8. Once the photo is uploaded, now you will check to see if all the words on your header can be seen and it fits the spot. You can reposition it a little, but sometimes, you may have to go back to Canva (or

whichever app you used) and create a size to better fit. I wish I could tell you it always fits, but it's not the case. Make sure to double check it. You can save changes and look at it, then still do an edit. This is why I mention to keep it private until you get it all set up to your liking.

9. The header is complete and now you can upload and schedule some of those graphics you made earlier.

10. You will go to the top bar where it says write something and click on it. On the box that pops up, click on the green photo icon in the long box at the bottom that says Add to your post. This will bring up your download file from your computer (on Mac, not sure about a PC) Choose your photo and then upload. Now you are ready to add the text above the graphic.

11. As you complete the upload and the text, now you will go to the bottom right of the post bar click on the small calendar on the bottom far right. Click here and this area allows you to set the date and time for whenever you want this post to go live in the Facebook group. If you don't have specific dates yet, schedule the post for two months after your launch date. Then once dates are set, you can go back into all those scheduled posts and reschedule them. You

can find this on the left column a little
more than half-way down.

You now have a Facebook Group only for the
launch of your book. If you don't have a Street Team
Group, you could use this at the end of the launch
session. This is another reason I recommend you don't
name the group Your Book Launch Team. If you do
change this to a Street Team Group at the end of the
launch, you'll need to remove all posts related to the
launch. If you have posted a graphic about the book
that is not date sensitive, you can leave that, but delete
all the posts in the thread below it. Remove all posts
and comments from team members.

I also recommend that you inform the current
launch team when the launch has concluded, the
group will become a Street Team. In this new group,
you will share more information than you do about
your writing and upcoming books than you do on your
author page. Let them have the option to stay or leave.
If they care to stay, they don't need to do anything. But
should they decide to leave, instruct them how to do
that. To do that, they need to go to the three dots up on
the upper right of the group. Click on the dots and a
drop-down menu pops up. Scroll down to the bottom
and they will see leave group. It will give them the
option to leave the group where they will click on it.

For our purpose now, we will use this Facebook
Group as your launch team hangout.

While you're here to create the Facebook group,

write the Welcome to the Team post and schedule it for two months after the launch date. This exercise will let you practice how to schedule posts, but don't worry, you will go back in when ready and edit this post to the proper date.

Here's a sample of one of the posts I've used to welcome the team:

Welcome to the BOOK TITLE Launch Team! I'm glad you're here! I appreciate your willingness to help me spread the word through graphics, various tasks, and honest reviews at the end of the Launch session. Thank you! Let's have some fun as we wait for everyone to join us here in our Facebook Group.

A couple questions to get to know each other as we spend the next few weeks together!

1. Where are you from?

2. What do you most look forward to this summer? (or proper season)

3. During this season, what's your favorite food or drink – or both?!

Don't be shy. I'll go first down in the thread below...

The above book had a summer launch date, so I chose the questions to go with that. I try to choose questions that might correspond with the book title or what the book is about when I can. Have a little fun and break the ice so they feel welcome, and you can get them ready.

Chapter 7

Create a Launch Team Application

You've already created the Google form header back in Chapter Five. Now you'll create your Launch Team Application in Google forms and will use that Header you've made. The template they have is pretty self-explanatory, and you can change it up somewhat. If you use another application for forms, go for it. It doesn't matter which company you use, what matters is the information you include in the application you'll send to people to apply for your launch team.

What to include in the Launch Team Application? Well, these applications vary as much as the folks who have a launch team. I've narrowed down the questions I ask on an application to help me obtain the important information I'm searching for in building a team. Some people are basic and ask for Name, Address and Email, while others ask a lot of questions on their form. Mine is not short, but is not the longest I've seen, that's for sure. Remember, this is your launch, and you can pick the items you want to use for your own launch. What I give you is my form I've used and adapted over that last several years to help the launch run smooth without having to send another email for information I could have gathered at the beginning.

Let's make a Launch Team Application on Google. In your Google apps section of your Google account (the gray dots by your photo or initial on the top right), click on the dots, scroll down for the triangle icon which will say drive and click on it. Up on the top left, you'll see a box with a plus sign and it says new. Click on that. Scroll down in the dropdown box to the purple icon that says Google forms and choose that. Go to the top left of the form where it says untitled form. Once you click here, you can fill in the name of your book and launch info, such as Your Book Name Launch Team Application. (Obviously, change the "Your Book Name" to your actual book name. You don't want all your launch applications to say the same thing. Change it for each launch you'll have.) This is a suggestion. You title this how you will know what it is.

You've now created a new form. Let's fill in all the details you'll need for this application. We'll start at the top and move our way down. We're going to upload the header which you've already created and downloaded to your computer. On the top right section, look for the symbol that is a painter's palette—the first one in the row of six icons before the purple Publish button. Click on the palette. This will give you a drop-down menu on the right side. The top line says theme. In this section, you will upload the header, change the font and size and the colors of the application. It will usually grab colors which are in your created header, but you can always change it up a bit more. Scroll down to the header section and click on the button that says image upload. Another small screen will pop up and will allow you to click on upload, then insert/done. The header will show up on the top of your launch application. Double check that all the details you want in that header are showing and are clear. If not, you will need to go back to Canva and fiddle with the header to get one the way you want it. After you make a couple, you get the hang of it and can eyeball it pretty close each time. Perfect for all your future books!

After the application header is complete, next you'll fill in the block under the header. If you place your cursor over the block and click, it enables the block to be changed. First thing—backspace where it says untitled form and type in Your Book Name Launch Team Application (or whatever you've named the form). Then move down to the form description. In this section, you will give the details of your book launch session. The important information needed in this block is when the book will release, when the launch session will happen, if you are giving the team a digital copy or paperback of the book to read, and what are some requirements or preferences to be on the team. And the important one you don't want to leave out—the date of the team selection and the date of notification. This is helpful to make in bold letters, so it will stand out for them to see. I do not send emails to everyone who applied and didn't make the team. Only a welcome to the team email to those I've selected. Be up front so you don't have to answer a lot of emails. You'll still get some asking if the team selection is complete, but a couple is better than all that applied.

It's important to let applicants know if they will receive a paperback or a digital copy if chosen for the team. I know a few launch managers require your team members buy the book to be on the team. Of all the book launches I've participated in so far, there's been less than five launch teams that have required that and a few of those know each other. My opinion, if you are going to ask someone to give up six to ten hours or more to read your book, then ask them to spend about six or seven weeks to help you promote the book, a free book —whether digital or paperback—is a nice gesture for their time and efforts. I am not a fan of requiring a team member purchase a book to participate.

You need to decide as your own book launch manager what your preference is. There isn't a perfect answer, but I know I'm hearing more and more team participants complain to me they will no longer do launches for authors or managers that require them to buy the book, share all the graphics, and leave a review.

To give a book, or require a team member to buy a book is something you must decide early on before you plan your team and create this application. They need to know in this application if you will send a book and what type—paperback or digital. Or if you will require a purchase of your book. Also on this application, you need to be clear as to what you hope they agree to do to help you launch. Curious, I polled some people on teams I have managed if they would have applied for the team if they had to buy the book. Across the board, they have said no—not as a requirement to be on the team. In my launch process, once the team has had the chance to read the book, I suggest, several times, if they liked the book, consider a purchase on launch day of a copy for a friend, an upcoming birthday or Christmas gift, a donation to the library or maybe for one of the little neighborhood pop-up library boxes. I've found they were very receptive to this idea and followed through with a purchase.

In the next section in this first box on the application, I bullet point the specific requirements I will use for the team. The first one is they must be on Facebook as that is where we will do most of our work. Others have tried to get people away from using Facebook because of the rumor that they sell data to Amazon and that's why Amazon deletes your reviews because they've found your launch team group and the names in it. I've not read anything where either side has admitted to that, but Facebook has worked for all the teams I've been a part of or managed over the last thirteen years. I will say, however, I do not name the Facebook Group with Your Book Name Launch Team should that be the case. No need to test the waters or draw attention to the little group that will only be around for about ten weeks until the group goes away.

The next requirement is they need to have at least one other social media account besides Facebook. The purpose is to spread the news about the book far and wide. Therefore, to have a team with a nice cross selection of social media sites is great.

Next, I ask them to commit to at least THREE TO FIVE promotional activities during the launch team session. I explain I will email a Task Checklist to the entire team with items they can choose from. Other than the non-negotiable one of posting an honest review on Amazon, I explain they are free to choose the other tasks off the list. Since I implemented this Task Checklist, many of the team members work hard to get all the items done to the best of their ability.

I also firmly request they must be willing to leave an honest Amazon review on launch day, or specified days during launch week, and they need to have an active account on Amazon (i.e., per Amazon, "You must have spent at least $50 on Amazon.com using a valid credit or debit card in the past 12 months."). There is little truth to the rumor that if you didn't buy the book to become a "verified purchase" Amazon will not approve your review. That is simply not true. I have been a part of over 400 launch teams and did not purchase all of those books. I have only had one review not approved and that was because I gushed over the author. The review is to be about the book. Once I re-read the Amazon guidelines, I rewrote the review only speaking about the book and it was accepted within twenty minutes. No other review has been rejected.

The last requirement is to share provided graphics on their social media accounts throughout the launch session.

In this section, you can also add your back cover blurb, especially if you will send the application out where maybe new-to-you readers may click on the application. This helps some decide if it's a story they would like to read and support.

That's all for that box. I know it's a lot. But necessary. However, there may be something else you'd like to include there. It's up to you. But it's best to keep the details short and easy to read through.

The text boxes that follow can be whatever you would like them to be. For me, the first boxes are for administrative purposes for emails, addresses to send the book if the list will go to a publisher, or if you're doing SWAG or drawings, you'll already have their contact info. My boxes are last name, first name, street address, city, state, and zip.

Then I get into the items I use to help me select a top-notch team. This is where I get into more of those social media details—what is your Facebook URL and number of followers, Instagram username and number of followers, and Twitter username and number of followers.

I finish up with a couple more text boxes:

Are you willing to share the graphics I will provide on your social sites?

If you have a website, podcast, or newsletter— would you be willing to spotlight the book and author?

Are you willing to not only post an honest review on Amazon, but are you willing to post reviews on other retail bookseller sites? (If you know where the book will be uploaded for sale, list it here. If you don't, it's alright to mention those closer to launch day within the Facebook Group and give the link to them.)

What is the name you use for leaving reviews on Amazon? I won't recognize you if you use CatLady246.

And the last two questions:

Why do you think you would make a great Launch Team member for this team? This section has come in handy when I need to choose between a couple of applicants to fill the team.

Do you have a creative idea or two in ways you would like to do to help promote the book? The answer here can often offer more ways they plan on supporting the book, such as reaching out to book clubs, sharing on their TikTok account of 19,000 (seriously had this!), and other various creative suggestions.

Once you are done with this form and have what you want in it to help you select your team, make sure you go to responses at the top of the form, click it and move the toggle to accepting responses. I didn't catch this once. I was out for the day and came home to seventy emails telling me they couldn't get into the application.

Make sure you do this step. Just saying!

Chapter 8

How Do I Find a Launch Team?

You've now created your application. You will go to the top of the form and right before the purple Publish box, click on the icon of a person and a plus sign for the drop-down menu. You will want to go down to the line under General Access where it says Responder view with the little globe in a circle icon. Make sure this is set to Anyone with the link. Click the Dark blue oval that says Done. Next go back up to the purple Publish box and click on that. Now it's ready to be used.

With the form created, you will be able to share it for people to apply. When you're ready to share the link, come back to this form, go up to those icons to the left of the purple Publish box and click on the link icon, next to the person/plus one at the right end. When you click on this link icon, it will create a long link for you to use. Underneath that long link is a box to check to shorten the URL, do that. This is the link to the application you will want everyone to use so you may gather all the information for the team in one place.

Often, I'll have authors gather names and emails from people when they're talking with them. This creates extra work for you, because you will have to go in and fill out the form or at the very least add their name and email to the Contact group. However, you'll be missing important information the form will be collecting for you. For instance, you're sending a little gift to each team member, now you'll have to email the person and get that information. Do yourself a favor, you will be very busy during the launch, you don't need extra chores to do, trust me. If you want to start a list of names and emails to send the form to later when closer to launch time, that would work. But trust me, adding ten to fifteen names and emails one-by-one into your contact list for the team, then going back to them to ask for the other information is a time killer for you. Been there, done that in the beginning of managing teams.

When you're ready to begin collecting the applicants and form a team, you copy and paste this application link into your newsletter, on your author page on Facebook if you have one, or any of your other social media sites and even share it in groups you are permitted to ask for launch team members. This is the one link to the application you will want all to use, so you may gather all the information for the team in one place. If people click that link to apply and submit this form, your Google form will collect all information for each applicant for you in one spot.

While you wait for the applications to come in, make sure your Facebook Group is ready for the selected team to join. The details on how to set up your Facebook Group were in Chapter Six. I wanted to keep this chapter on how to find the launch team. However, while you wait, now is the perfect time to write the post to include with a graphic that says Welcome to the Team and get it scheduled for the date you know you will email those new team members.

Create the first graphic you will have them share and schedule that in the Facebook Group. I usually create the first one to say Coming Soon! This graphic includes the book and the date of release, the book's hashtag, and the author's website. Once you make it, schedule this one also so you are ready. While you're in the Group uploading this, make sure you look at any scheduled posts you have and change any dates on those you've pre-set in the future. Now's the time to put the correct date on them if you haven't already.

I suggest you use this small quiet time to get that first week ready for you as you hit the ground running with the team.

Once the application period has ended, you will go back to the application form and click on the purple publish box. At the top of this drop-down box where it says Accepting responses, move the toggle to close the responses by sliding it to the left. Then move to the bottom of the box and click on Save.

To view and download your response spreadsheet, in the middle of the bar above the form it says Questions, Responses and Settings. Click on Responses. In the drop-down from there, you can choose to Download responses (.csv). This will give you the spreadsheet with all the names of people who have applied. The reason to have a spreadsheet is to keep all the information separated and in boxes to move them out of your way when you want to work with just a column or two of the information.

This new spreadsheet is what you'll work through until you find your 35-50 team members if you have more than 50 people apply. Too few and you won't capture many reviews. Over fifty and I feel you're giving away sales. Please know that you can't and shouldn't count on 100 percent of the team to leave a review. But if you do your best, they can give you a large amount. Some of the reviews will also come from people who get free books from book sources such as NetGalley if you're a traditionally published author. And if you did preorders and had graphics for your team to share about those? Yes, those folks may leave reviews, too. Don't get fixated on the 50 reviews. Work on marketing your book and utilizing your launch team while you have them at this time.

Before you look through the data to choose your team, I recommend making a second copy of the spreadsheet to leave the original untouched should you need to go back to it. Next, slide the divider lines all the way to the left to cover names, addresses and emails. I do not want to see names now, as I'm looking for the best fit. That way, I don't see a name I recognize and let it tempt me to not follow my process. Right now, your concentration is to find:

Did they follow directions?

Are they on Facebook—the number one requirement?

Are they on at least one other social media site?

Are they eligible to leave Amazon reviews?

Since this is a copy of the entire list of applicants and their information, you can delete those who don't meet those criteria above if you have more than enough people who have applied. If you don't have over fifty, I say highlight the rows in red of applicants who may not have met the requirements you're looking for such as active on Facebook, able to post on Amazon, or don't have a decent number of followers or reach. This way they are still there if you decide to pull them in to fill the team anyway. Then you'll compare the Facebook numbers. However, if they aren't on Facebook, they need to be deleted anyway as they won't be able to receive your graphics or other information you share there.

Now that you've sorted through, those left should have met the above most important criteria. Next comes the time where you will look at numbers in the sense of will there be a good cross section of reach between Facebook, Twitter and Instagram. While you might look at someone's submission and they have nineteen people on Instagram, that's not an automatic no. They may have 8,000 on Twitter. You're looking to balance the numbers between those columns of social media reach using all the applicants. Those that jump out with large numbers on all three social media sites, highlight that row in green—because they are a GO! You want to have a good reach of social media numbers between the members of your team.

As I look through the spreadsheet to highlight who I'll choose, first I check to make sure people haven't signed up twice. It happens, every time. Then I begin the process of going through the list and make sure everyone has said they're on Facebook, if not, delete those. In one of the classes I taught, someone asked, "But what if they have super high numbers everywhere else, they just don't use Facebook, can't I use them anyway?" My answer was, "You sure can. Remember though, you said that was a requirement and they didn't follow directions. Also, you will now have to send that one person every graphic or message or drawing announcement, etc. as well as post the information in the Facebook Group. One person. If you have the extra time to remember to do that, then go for it. That's a decision only you can make because only you know your time and schedule."

Spreadsheet is now cleaned up and you're ready to sort through the rest and highlight them like a traffic light—green for a definite yes or go, yellow for maybe and red for probably not, mostly because of very low numbers of followers. Once you have gone through the entire spreadsheet, count the green. If you have your full amount (35-50) that you want, there's your team. But maybe you only have 24 green, next you'll go through the yellow and choose as many from there as you can or want. Should you need to go into the highlighted red grouping, look for the highest numbers you can for this. For example, if you're light on Instagram numbers overall, do any of the red highlighted people have a decent number there? That's what you'll look for.

Once you've chosen your fifty members, delete those you've decided against for this particular launch. Now slide the columns you've hidden on the left back open with their information. From this, I suggest you do a copy and paste of the names, addresses and emails into an Excel sheet (or your choice of log) for ease of contact. But don't delete the entire sheet. Save this entire spreadsheet in your Google form for this book's launch team info. Once you have the team chosen on that copied spreadsheet and have deleted the folks not on the team, use that sheet to add the team members' emails to your email system. Whether you have an email set up for all your books or an email for each individual book, import all those email addresses so you're ready to go with the team's Welcome to the Team email. I prefer to create a separate contact list for each book in the email account which allows me to know what book they were part of. I use Gmail for this, and can upload the list of names into my contacts by book name for ease every time I want to send info to only that team.

You've finally whittled the spreadsheet down to your top fifty (or number of your choice) members, now you're ready to get started working with the team.

That first bit of launch team business is to send the people you have selected a welcome to the team email and attach the link to the Facebook group for them to click over and join. Like I said above, I use Gmail for the launch team mail system and some documents, but you decide which email carrier you will use. Make sure you have all the names and emails added to whatever system you're using though. I prefer to set up each of the teams as separate contact lists. This will help you a great deal with your subsequent book launches if you do the same. You won't be scrolling down through your contact list looking for the exact people for the particular book launch you're working on. You'll click the exact email list for that book.

When you send any emails to your team, unless it is only to one team member, be sure to use the Blind Carbon Copy or BCC feature. It's not appropriate to email fifty people and all of their personal emails show for everyone to see. They've entrusted you with that information. Be respectful and don't forget to use the BCC. Besides, who wants to scroll down through fifty names to get to the actual body of the email?

Below is a sample of one of the Welcome to the Team letters I've used to give you an idea of what you could put in your letter. Of course, you will change the generic words throughout the letter in all caps and also make it your own with your personality. There is a paragraph about when the team will receive their book. Please change that to the proper delivery date of your book, whether you will send the Digital or the publisher will send a paperback. If it will be a digital book, how they will receive this: PDF, NetGalley or Book Funnel. Special note here, if you're publisher will be using NetGalley for the team, make sure you add a line on the application that says—email address used for your NetGalley account. Often people have a different email for this account but can't figure out why the link you gave them won't let them get the book. Most of the times it's because they gave you a different email than the one they use for their NetGalley account.

A sample for a Welcome to the Team letter:

Congratulations! You've made the Launch Team for BOOK TITLE by AUTHOR. This is book #X in the XYZ Series. (If applicable)

I want to welcome you to the Team. Over the next several weeks, we will work together to help launch this book. I'll be giving you helpful tips and graphics to help you—help me—share about this book.

I will assist you by giving you the information through emails from this email address, and over in the Launch Team Facebook Group every week. I promise not to flood your inbox. We will work from the Facebook Group, so it's very important you join us there, promptly. You can count on at least one to two posts in the Facebook Group each week from me. Make sure you have your notifications set to receive all notifications for the next several weeks in this Launch Team Group as well as checking your Junk folder if you're not hearing from me through emails.

Your first task as a member of this team is to click on the link below and go request to join the NAME OF LAUNCH TEAM FACEBOOK GROUP. Once there, you will see a post to introduce yourself. Please do! Let's see where everyone is from!

Here's that link: (GET THE HYPERLINK FROM THE FACEBOOK GROUP URL AND USE THE LINK OPTION THROUGH YOUR EMAIL PROVIDER.)

I look forward to spending some fun time with you over this launch session for this book.

If you ever have questions, or need help with posting, please email me, or create a separate post in the Facebook Group so I see it. I'll do my best to help you figure out the issue!

One last thing, your names and addresses, which you filled out on your application, went to my publisher and you should receive your book soon. (If you're traditionally published and publisher provides books or NetGalley/Book Funnel links) But there will be some activities we will do in the meantime to get us ready for Launch Day, MONTH DATE, 20XX that won't require you've finished reading the book.

Let's get ready to have some fun. Again, welcome to the BOOK TITLE Launch Team.

See you over in the Facebook Group!

. . .

In the Welcome to the Team letter, I include the Hyperlink to the Facebook Group. Here's how to do that for your letter:

Go to your Facebook Group.

1. Go all the way to the top in the search bar that says facebook.com and click on that bar.
2. Copy that link. It will be the link to your Facebook Group.
3. Come back to your email and find the icon for adding a link and click on that. (It looks like a chain link, split in half.)
4. Follow the prompts in your email provider and paste that Facebook Group link in there.
5. Depending on your email service, you can rename the link instead of the one you will get with Facebook and a lot of numbers. I like to use the group name I've created for that launch. It doesn't matter, the link will take your team to the proper group. This way they don't have to go searching for what you might have called the launch group.

Give the members a few days to click over. I recommend you pop in often these first couple of days to watch who has joined in. You'll have to approve their requests. If you have done a welcome to the team graphic and asked them a couple of questions, be sure to comment on every one who follows your prompt to introduce themselves. Nothing worse than when you walk into a party and the host never gets around to at least acknowledge that you have arrived. Start the engagement from the get go.

After a few days, if you see that a few have not joined, it's okay to send a note to those folks. I've had to send a few. If there's a few of them, send it without a name in the first line and remember to use the BCC again.

Here's what I've sent:

Good morning, MEMBER'S NAME! (Or leave off if sending to several team members.)

I mentioned in your welcome letter about the Facebook Group. We will work mostly from there, so it's very important you join us this week. I've noticed you haven't joined the team over in the group and wanted to reach out to you.

Your first task as a member of this team is to click on the link below and go request to join the BOOK TITLE Launch Team Facebook Group. Maybe you missed the email, so I've included the link again. Once there, you will see a post to introduce yourself. Please do.

Here's that link again: (PUT THAT HYPERLINK IN AGAIN.)

I look forward to spending some fun time with you over this launch session for my book, BOOK TITLE. However, if you can no longer participate in this launch, let me know. Life happens and something may have changed in your schedule since you applied. I understand. I ask that you let me know so I won't send you further information

If you have questions, please email me.

Thanks.

Often, once I send the above email, the folks are apologetic and said they read it and forgot to follow through. Only once or twice did I have someone say they had changed their mind or got too busy to take part. Email for a nudge. It's much better to know if those stragglers still plan to participate or have moved on and didn't inform you.

Chapter 9

Keeping Track of Team Actions

KEEPING track of what the team does is helpful if you will use the information for a drawing or a big grand prize at the end. This list can also be helpful for you when you do your next book launch. You'll be able to look through the key points you wanted help on and see whether they did those activities. What a great resource to glance through the list when you choose your next team to see if names repeat and assess if they were active in your launch from the previous book. This has become a tool I rely on for each team I do with repeat authors.

On teams I've managed, I now recognize names in applications that I know what their participation level was without looking back on preview logs. Some of those who are great participants will get an automatic green highlight. Those that got the book, came to Facebook, and that's about it will get the automatic red highlight. Time saved on team selection, for sure.

The Excel spread sheet I create to keep track of team actions I call Task Log. Down the left side of the sheet are their names, last name first. Across the top are the key activities I want the team to do. I take these items from my Task Checklist, which I will explain in Chapter Ten. I don't take all the items listed, but those items that are most important to me. With this list, I can go through the Facebook Group and check the box with an X of an item they have done off the list. I have asked them to do the task or share the graphic, and then come back and let me know they've done it in the thread below the post. This makes it quick to find their work.

I've printed the list to mark off tasks, and I've left it on the computer and go back and forth between the Facebook Group and the Task Log sheet online. Whichever works for you is the best way. To me, this sheet has proven over and over to me it's well worth the extra time to keep track of the team members. If you're dedicated to writing more books, you'll thank yourself down the road that you started this habit of keeping track of team member activities right from the start. You may even create a log for your team that works better for you and what you're keeping track of. Then create a template you can copy and paste into a new document with each of your book launches.

Below are the checkbox titles on the spreadsheet I've created for what I feel is most important for my use. Use this as a starting point to build your own log should you choose to do this. You may add more to your list. Here's my list:

1. I want to know if they've done the first requirement—Have they joined the Facebook Group?
2. Did they write an Amazon review?
3. Have they shared graphics?
4. Posted other reviews on other sites?
5. Wrote a blog post or sent in their newsletter?
6. Purchased a copy?
7. And I leave a blank for "other"—something they did, and they informed me of.

Although at the end of each launch team session I manage, I send out a Task List Check-in and survey, I still take the time to keep track of their weekly tasks and use this spreadsheet. That way, at the end, when I do a recap of the team activities, I'm not starting from scratch to pull these stats together. To be honest, the first time I did this, I wondered if I was admitting to my detail-oriented, overachieving self-tendencies' and was wasting time. Now several dozen managed teams later, I'm grateful for those first spreadsheets since I now see repeat applicants and am able to make a quick decision about some of them.

I will note, I no longer use my original spreadsheet, it had more categories on it than I needed to make my member choices. It's your decision on what you're looking for in a qualified team member. Trust me, it's more than someone told me they want to help, so I'll let them be on the team. To have strong parameters for your team will provide a solid team, launch after launch.

Chapter 10

Make Sure They are Informed

No MATTER what task you ask the team to do, make sure you keep them informed on how to do it properly. Don't assume they know what you mean by share the graphic. In each launch I start, the first graphic I have them share—Coming Soon!—someone will ask me to make the graphic sharable as they aren't able to share it to their Facebook profile. You can count on this if they haven't done a share from a group. They may ask if it doesn't work because they are working on a PC.

When this happens, problem is often that they don't know how to download the graphic to their computer, and share on their own social media. I cut right to the issue with that first graphic. In my text above this first graphic I post, I give the instructions to download the graphic to their computer, and share that graphic to their social media sites. I explain that none of us can share a graphic from a group. It's how Facebook groups work. Facebook will not allow shares from a private group for the privacy of each person in the group. I assure them they're doing fine.

In each step or request I give the team, I do my best to set them up for success. I not only ask them to do something, but I educate, equip, and encourage them on the task.

Another one of the first few items of business I do with a launch team is to ask them to set their notifications to receive all notifications from the Facebook group. I have a screenshot of the notifications box they will get off the drop-down box in the group. I have a Word document with instructions how to do this which I copy and paste above the screenshot I've set to post. Although, on occasion, I receive an email that Facebook shows different directions on a person's screen than what I posted, so I recommend you check it from time to time to see if the location is the same.

This is the wording I use that I place in the text above the screenshot:

Good afternoon, Team!

Just a quick housekeeping note for you today. Make sure you change your notifications in the group so you will see all the posts in here. Yes, for a few weeks, you'll get all our posts and comments. But then after launch week, it will stop! So, hang in there, please?

If you've never done this, here are the instructions:

1. In our group, on the top right under the blue Invite Box there are three little gray dots. Click on those.

2. On the drop-down menu, click on Manage Notifications, four down with a bell icon.

3. Select All Posts right under the In-app notifications.

4. Then click Save on the bottom line!

This will allow you to receive notifications of what I will share here in the Private Team Group.

Thanks!

Next up, book reviews. I want to inform the team about how to do a proper book review. I created my sheet of helpful tips for writing reviews to make sure the reviews would have a better chance of not being rejected. There are certain reasons for rejection, so if we can make sure they know them ahead of time, we can stay on the positive side to have more reviews accepted. Though, to be honest, none of us can guess what new reason a review will receive a rejection.

When I wrote the sheet, I wrote it with the first-time reviewer in mind. The tips I use are clear to me, but for someone writing a review for the first time, maybe not. The list has complete details in the hope there would be less chance for not understanding what needed to be done. Below is my current review sheet I send to my launch teams. You are welcome to use this as a basis to write your own sheet with your wording and personality. Should you decide to copy my entire Book Review Sheet, I ask you to leave my name on the sheet as it is my creation. Thanks!

Tips for Writing Your Launch Team Book Review

By Tammy Karasek – The Launch Team Geek!

Book reviews are important to an author and to the success of a book more than you can imagine. THANK YOU for your part in the Launch Team to reach our book review goals! Whether this is your first book review or your tenth, I've created this helpful sheet for you to use in your book review process. Don't let the long list scare you. It's my hope to answer questions you may have in writing that review for our author and the reader trying to decide to buy the book or not!

Once you receive and finish the book, write your review and save it in a Word document or somewhere you can copy and paste it when it's time to post. If you write your review in Goodreads, they allow early reviews and it will be one of your reviews complete. Then you'll be able to copy and paste it to other sites from there. This will set you up for success for your honest Amazon review post at launch time, too! You can use the same review on all sites. If the site asks for a title, change the title up a bit if you'd like.

A review only needs to be a few sentences. Do NOT write a long summary of the book, copy and paste the back cover blurb, or copy and paste the book description at the top of the listing on Amazon. By the time readers make it to the reviews, they already know what the book is about. They need the review of what the reader thought of the book.

THIS IS IMPORTANT! DO NOT REVEAL in any way that you know the author. DON'T say the author is my friend, neighborhood, relative, etc. Your review WILL NOT get published.

DO NOT say anything about the author at all. I've had team members' reviews rejected because of this. The review is on the book, not the author. Once I told them to remove the author, the review was up within twenty to thirty minutes. It's in Amazon's guidelines, it's about the book, not the author. Don't risk the rejection.

You can say you know the author or served on the launch team in a review on your blog. Doing so adds value to the review on your blog because of your personal connection. BUT only on a blog post.

What should the review say? Rate the book with your honest thoughts. If you loved it and think it's worth reading, then put five stars and tell readers what you liked about the book. Also, did you learn from it? Was there a quote or line you keep thinking about it? You can add that into your review. Readers do want to know what you thought about the book and if you would recommend it to them. And why?

If you'd like to add a photo on a review site that allows it, DO NOT USE a Launch Team photo. You can share a photo of the book that you take holding it, just not one you've created for the launch or one of the Launch Team graphics provided for you.

Post reviews as soon as you finish reading the book. Create one review, then copy and paste it on the other sites accepting reviews. DO NOT POST ON AMAZON until Launch Day. They won't accept it until then, anyway, so don't try and think they've rejected you.

If you did *not* purchase a book, please end your reviews with a statement something like this, in your own words: "Disclaimer: I received this book from the publisher and was not required to leave a review. The opinion is my own."

Not sure what to write? Read through other book reviews. Don't let the long reviews intimidate you—these are unnecessary. Less is best! In fact, most people won't read a long review.

Bottom line, *please* post your honest reviews.

To have this instructional sheet created before your launch session gives you more time to interact with the team and have some fun as well. This will also be a perk for your future launches when this is ready to be used at the time for reviews in your launch session. Any item you can prepare and save in a file to use as needed will be handy. Your future launch self will be grateful you did this.

A note for you on using those reviews left by your team members after the launch. I recently learned something about this and want authors to be aware of the issue. I was told an author can't copy and paste a review from Amazon and use it in their social media. Being the *why* girl that I am, I began to dig through the depths and files of Amazon to see if this is true. It wasn't easy to find, but I stuck it out to find that it is, in fact, true. And false. Ah, don't you love those types of answers?

First, let me state, I am not a lawyer nor do I play one on tv. My information came from almost two hours of digging through legal websites, amazon's site, and any anywhere else I found the topic discussed.

It is true that you should not copy and paste a book reader's review and use it on your personal social media in the promotion of your book. It goes back and forth between the intellectual property infringement and fair use of said review. However, on more than one occasion, I found where you *could* use a full review, *IF* you asked—and were granted—permission from the original review writer. However, Amazon does have an understood and non-exclusive right to use the reviews anywhere they choose within their website. But as an author of the book, you don't have that right to that review. Amazon claims ownership of the review on their site.

The other comment found on a legal site was that you could use a small portion, or phrase in a review if using it in a positive way. Otherwise, if you wanted to use more, you would need to reach out to the reviewer and ask permission to use their review. And . . . get that in writing.

However, if you are doing a launch team and will create and use the application to join the team form, you could add a section to your application with the Yes or No option and wording something like this:

I give permission to AUTHOR to use all or part of my review from any website I choose to leave a review for the purpose to promote their book.

This way, you have permission from the beginning of the launch. Make sure to save those applications especially for this reason.

Another option is to grab a couple phrases from several reviews and place them on a graphic around your book on the graphic.

Chapter 11

Create a Task List for Your Team

A FEW YEARS BACK, when I first managed teams, I would have a couple of team members ask if they could do more to help the author. Ideas like share with their book club, ask a school library to put one on their shelf, have the author on their podcast and more. Consistent questions by various team members gave me the idea to create a Task Check List they can work on throughout the launch session. Although I grab my top items from the list and set those apart to focus on for Task Tuesday, I figured since they continued to ask, I would give them a list of ideas. Therefore, the Task Check List came to be a part of each launch. I've noticed since I implemented the list, the actions have increased within the groups.

The list is one page, and while I don't insist they do all the items on the list, I've gathered tasks I see can help them keep the buzz about the book ongoing throughout the launch. I put the ones I would appreciate they do at the top of the list. You can use this list if you want to do a contest and give a prize for the most completed items at the end of the session. Some participants are all about a competition, others won't do anything as they either don't like a competition or think they won't win anyway, so why bother. If you make it a competition, be prepared to have enough gifts as many will work for those prizes.

This may sound like I'm not sure of which of these you should do, but it's more that I want you to understand there are different personalities on every team. It's your launch, and you need to decide what and how you want to do it and then stand firm and promote it with enthusiasm. But beware of the strong personalities who may give pushback and hold you back from what you want to achieve. Some teams do great with contests. The next team will ignore the challenges and share without entering the drawings. You never know.

In Excel, I've created this task list, but you can make your list wherever you choose. It can be a Word document or even as fun and fancy as a list created in Canva. From time to time, I may add an idea or two depending on the author, the ideas the author wants to use, especially if much of the launch team is local. If that's the case, the author may suggest the team share a flyer for a local meet and greet or the launch party if it will accommodate a group.

I use the following items most of the time. Please note, this is my template, so where you see, insert date, insert book, etc.—those will be your dates, book title, and your name.

Hi Team,

Download this Task Checklist to give you ideas of other ways to help with the launch of this book!

1. Read, NAME OF BOOK PRIOR to release day!

2. Post a review on Amazon DURING LAUNCH DAY – INSERT DATE.

3. The month before release, post reviews on sites like Goodreads, BookBub, and others that allow pre-release reviews.

4. Share about NAME OF BOOK on your social sites at least three times during release week – INSERT DATES.

5. Post a photo of you with your ARC or digital/iPad copy on your social media and say something about it, then post on the team page under the Task thread with Done.

6. Share the preorder graphic, then post on the team page under the Task thread with Done. (Use only if you have a preorder option)

7. While waiting for your book, mark INSERT BOOK on your Goodreads account as *To Read*, then follow that up with *Read* when you complete the book.

8. Share graphics I created on your social accounts. Tag AUTHOR NAME so I can see it with @AUTHOR NAME. Don't forget the hashtag for the book, too.

9. Share graphics on other social media sites about reading that you're a part of, like Avid Reader of Christian Fiction, etc. Also book clubs! But please make sure you may do so!

10. Recommend NAME OF BOOK to your local library or local independent bookseller. You may need to reach out to the librarian for your county or state to request they purchase the book now.

11. Love the book? Please consider buying a copy on launch day for a friend or someone you think would love it, too!

12. Do a mini review of the book on Facebook or Instagram.

13. Share about NAME OF BOOK when it goes on sale, there's a giveaway, etc.

14. If you have a blog, newsletter, or podcast, would you consider an interview with AUTHOR NAME?

15. Create a graphic of NAME OF BOOK and share on the Launch Team group—also share on your own social media sites!

16. Think of ten friends who might be interested in this book and send them an

email with the link to buy the book on Amazon or any other bookseller the book is listed with.

17. Leave a review on Barnes & Noble, Christian Book, Books A Million, Target, BookBub, Kobo, Library Thing. If you use other locations where you can post book reviews, do those as well. (Make sure you list where your book will be listed for sale. Make it easy for them to go find spots to leave those honest reviews.

By having a handy checklist the team can print out, and your encouragement to do the tasks on the list, your book has a greater chance to garner more attention than just on social media. That is what we want. Word-of-mouth recommendations often instigate the best sales.

If other options come to mind, add them to your list. You can add those items for your upcoming launch, but don't add more to the list throughout a current launch. Make notes of items you've thought of and add to your master sheet for the next time. Although you could use a new idea on one of your Task Tuesday's during a current launch to see what kind of reaction the team receives if they do the item. I wouldn't recommend you add it to the Task List and resend it to the team. Sending them another list may confuse them and they may wonder if this is another list of more tasks to do—or do again. However, like I said above, you could create a graphic of that new task and put the graphic up for a Task Day for them to do.

Chapter 12

How Much is Too Much?

WILL it be obvious if you are asking the team to do too much? Don't worry, they'll tell you in one of two ways. Or both. The first is by complaining to you. They may tell you they didn't realize there would be so much work in helping with your launch. The other is even worse. They will quit, walk away and never tell you they've moved on. They won't respond to emails or be present in the Facebook Group.

On the flip side of too much is the point of too little. They won't be able to assist you in sharing the great news that your book is ready to release if you don't equip them with the graphics to share, ideas to tell others about your book or even get them excited about your book after they've read it. Your silence will create their silence.

Over the fourteen years I've taken part in launch teams, I've been a part of some that sent so many emails with graphics I couldn't keep up. Another few sent no graphics at all and when asked if they would create graphics for us to share, the authors informed us they thought that's what the launch team did. Still others sent very little and didn't interact with us at all. We didn't have a Facebook Group, didn't receive emails, or instructions where to find graphics to share.

Then there were the dynamic teams that created graphics and shared them one or two per week within the Facebook Group so we could download and share. The small amount spaced over the launch period allowed us the chance to get them done, not overwhelm our schedules and not overkill our readers with the same book four to five times a week with posts about the book. Repetition can be good, but every day is not a great thing for this.

The worst team I was ever on taught me to never be a part of that particular author's launch again. Ever. This author sent us an email twice a week to remind us to go to the Facebook Group and see what new items they posted for us to share. In the Facebook Group, there were two graphics shared per day. Every. Day. Yes, two graphics, seven days per week for five weeks. And a Facebook Live three days a week—to remind us to do the work. When asked about her massive number of requests, she replied that with the short launch time, she needed the information out there as much as it could be. Which was unfortunate she thought this. It created the opposite. The team dropped out quick.

However, this can go the opposite direction of how much is too little? Short launch team participation of three to four weeks (or less, I've seen) does not give the time to build the excitement and buzz you want for your book. There's not as much opportunity for preorders, which helps the publisher see what to expect for print. This also shows the marketing companies what book is hot for this publication month. With the right number of shares about the book, we have a much greater chance for people to see the excitement about the book and then want to purchase the book.

We need to remember, social media is a fluctuating medium. Even though someone posted something this morning, the news feed continues to scroll and add new information. So having the graphics by a few people over two or three weeks may not grab much attention. Our goal is for people to see the book over a few weeks in as many places as we can. Social media is a great marketing tool to share what's new, what's happening and what do I need. Being able to post five or more graphics over a several week period gives you a greater chance that folks will see your book. Add to that, the other actions the team will work at spreading the news equals more opportunities for preorders and sales.

I've watched many teams over the years. The shorter length launch sessions don't always get enough airtime. Three or four graphics shared, the book released, and the opportunity to get the book in front of people slows down quite a bit. Now it becomes the next effort in marketing your book of finding new and creative ways to share about it. Not impossible at all, but the thrill of something new and shiny has waned somewhat.

In my many years of experience, I've found the best success for the authors' teams I manage has been with the six to eight-week period. The first week is getting the team into the Facebook Group. Giving them their first graphic to share at the end of that week, which is the "Coming Soon!" graphic I've created and provided. This graphic I used for two reasons. The first is that I can make sure everyone knows how to download a graphic from a group. The next is to grab hold of their excitement that I selected them for the launch team.

A day or two after I've given them a graphic to share, I will go to my profile and put in the hashtag for the book I instructed them to use. I see what pops up and check out how they are sharing the graphic and words they've used. I provide them with a statement to copy and paste or tell them they may use their own words to share with their friends. My personal motto is in play here again—educate, equip, and encourage the team.

The first week is slow, allowing all to jump into the group. Starting week two, the twice per week posts in the Facebook Group, an occasional email with instructions will keep the team engaged. With this basic model, I've not heard one complaint about too much work.

Working with the team over the next seven weeks has shown a good return for the team's effort. I believe I've found a sweet spot to work with a team with the right amount of launch actions. Kind of like little Miss Goldilocks—not too hot, not too cold, but just right.

Chapter 13

Interacting with Your Team

YOUR INTERACTIONS WITH THE TEAM, without a doubt, will set the tone for the entire launch. Whatever tone or personality you bring to the group grabs the team and they act upon that.

I realize some authors are reserved. Others may be full of energy and are a party waiting to happen. Ahem, like the author of this book!

However, don't let this deter you from communicating with the team. After all, *you* are part of this launch team as well. I suggest you don't drop in each day and say something. A couple times a week works fine. You can like their posts, comment on a graphic someone made to share or just drop a graphic in the group that says Thank You. Remind them it's not a graphic to share, it's from you to each of them. After all, who doesn't like their efforts to make a difference and be appreciated?

You could do a surprise Facebook Live that is

recorded and stays there in the group for the members to view as they come in. You could also do a YouTube instructional video on explaining the task list you sent to them that day and post it in the group. One of those Facebook Lives could be for you to share where your story idea came from. You need to remember when they received the book before you talk too much about the story, though. You don't want to share any spoilers. Many readers love to have the details of the hidden meanings within a book. I've watched enough of the Facebook Lives with authors and their team to grasp there is a genuine interest in the behind-the-scenes information.

Some questions I've received to ask the author were: What did you learn from writing this book? What's your favorite scene you wrote in this book? Where did your idea come from for it? Is there a particular character in the book based on someone you are close to? Remember, readers are interested.

Another topic to discuss with the team could be about your writing process and you take a walk around your writing spot or office with your laptop, or even the coffee shop where you'll work on that next book.

Interaction means engagement, which translates into excitement to share about your book with all friends and family the launchers can. They get as excited about your book as you are, because you took the time to include them in your life. They feel you are their friend, and friends want to help friends as best they can.

Knowing more about you, your writing process and your favorite writing spots allows them to be an insider and with that, they can become your greatest asset—a fan eager to join in over in your Street Team Private Group. These particular members are there for the long haul most times. They want you to write more books. When you show up to your Street Team group and keep them informed of what's going on in your writing world, at your fingertips will be a great resource to gather folks for your next launch team.

Remember though, interact with your launch team a little each week somehow. There is no reason to post a message every day—please don't—but it's important to go through and like a post, leave a comment and answer questions you might see as prompt as you can. They may ask how to do something, and if you answer in a week or two, they may not bother to complete the task.

The easiest way to remember to engage—these are your friends for the next six to seven weeks. Pull up a chair and enjoy their company at the table. Don't sit back in silence and watch, nor should you talk their ear off. But please let your presence be known.

Chapter 14

Facebook Live, Zoom or Nothing

WOULDN'T it be wonderful to meet up with your launch team in person? But it's almost impossible. Your team members will come from all over the country, or all over the world, if you allow participation from those folks.

We are fortunate to have tools to aid in the ability to visit with a team. One is Zoom and everyone can take part in real time and, if set up to do so, everyone may participate. This allows people the choice to keep all but the host on Mute and use the Chat feature to leave questions. Or stay muted but raise a hand and let you, the host, call on them to unmute and speak.

I don't recommend everyone stay unmuted. If it's only a couple of you, it might be okay. If it's a large group of the team, just don't. Someone's dog will bark, a child or spouse may scream in the background, or anything you can imagine. I'm sure all of us could share a Zoom story or two now because of how many Zoom calls we've all had since 2020.

Another tool is Facebook Live. This happens in the Facebook group, but only the host can talk. This is best when you, the author, only want to pop in, leave an announcement or message, and go. Here, you can ask team members to send their questions ahead of the call and you answer them during the Facebook Live, which is a good option.

However, I've seen Facebook Lives where the author says a few items, then opens it up for members to post their questions in the thread below the Live. Then the author must continue to scroll down the feed to see the questions. I don't think authors realize some of them lean into their screen to read on their laptop. By leaning into their screens, they pitch their head back to watch and read. I can't tell you how many noses I've had the privilege of seeing up close and personal. Up being the operative word. There's a visual for you, right? However, you could choose to let someone monitor your comment thread and text you the questions only, that can work well. And no more nose views.

Either of these can be useful. Knowing the best time to do either is the tricky part. Remember, your team of folks may be in several time zones. You'll need to consider some may work during the day. Should you decide to do either of these, an evening may be best and make sure you record the event. This allows those to view the recorded message when their schedule allows. With all of this in mind, as far as a day and time, you could poll the team and tell them you will choose one that has the most votes but you will record the session for others to view at their convenience.

To be honest, some of these have been fun and well-attended. Yet, they also seem to rise and fall within a team's interest. One team may love them and half the team shows up every time you do a call. The next team only you and one other team member may show up for the event. You could try a Zoom call and a Facebook Live and see how the team reacts to each of them.

One author I work with often has Zoom calls that are a blast. We use this at the end of the launch as a thank you, some fun, and a sendoff to the team. I send out an email with our date selected and the link for the Zoom call. This is done the week after launch day. In that email, I ask them to send me questions they would like the author to answer.

I explain these questions could be anywhere from what the next book will be and its release date to who's the author's favorite author. I've even been asked: I've learned many writers are snackers as they write, are you and if so, what's your favorite snack to munch as you write? So many of the team members often ask, is there someone in real life you based this character from? With the time given to the team to think about what they'd like to learn, we can receive some fun questions.

In these end-of-launch Zoom calls, we've added in

some drawings from data collected through the launch such as who had the most posts in the group, who created their own graphics, who shared the most graphics, or who completed the Final Task Checklist and sent it in with the most items completed. With this one though, we plan for more than one winner, which could be a $5.00 to $10.00 ecard to Amazon, Visa Card, Chick-fil-A or Starbucks or Chick-fil-A. You decide and include this in your launch budget. My caution to you is to choose an ecard the person will be able to use in their area. One author wanted me to email the recipients for their choices of about six companies. This worked great.

Please don't think I want to deter you from these types of activities. My point is to make you aware that you'll need to be determined in your promotion of either of them to the team, and you will need to do something to entice them to come join in. You will need more than just your smile and the question, "So, any questions for me?" If planned with attention to details, Facebook Lives and Zoom calls can be a lot of fun.

I caution you with this ... if the thought of carrying the conversation for a while as they warm up is already making you break out in hives, this might be something you pray and ponder over before diving in.

Chapter 15

Launch Party Online or In Person —or Both!

I'LL BE the first to admit, I love any reason to plan a party! A friend long ago informed me she felt I was just a party waiting to happen, so I have a couple party ideas for you. Yet you might wonder how could you do a party when your team spans the country, or world. Easy. You do an online, in person or both.

When you launch your book, you are giving attention to a brand-new book. We writers often refer to it as birthing a book baby. To be honest, it takes at least nine months to get this book ready to be launched out. So, after all that work, the book is now ready to be birthed —to announce it has arrived. Why not celebrate it? And who best to celebrate it with than your launch team and your friends and family local who cheered you on in this journey? Much like a baby shower, but with a book, we anticipate the arrival—then gather to share it with others who were supportive of your hard work.

Let's break it down to the three launch party suggestions. One: online with your launch team only. Two: in person for those who live close enough to join in the festivities. Three: combine the two with a big double party—well, for at least part of the time. Let's dig deeper on all three.

The online party could be for your launch team only. Much like I described the Zoom call, send off at the end of the last chapter. This is a Zoom Call on launch day. You send the Zoom Call link to the entire team days in advance. You hype it up and let them get excited and know what to expect. If you plan to do several drawings and a Grand Prize, tell them. Be creative. You might even play a game or two asking them questions about the book. First to respond with the correct answer wins a small prize. If this is your style, this could be a fun time to thank the team for all they did for your launch. Make it fun with them and inform them the book launch session is complete, if this is when you've decided they may be done.

Next, you can do a local party. You might set up an in-person launch/book signing party at an independent bookseller in your city. Or rent a room in your church, city recreation center, or maybe the coffee shop you wrote most of the book—you know, your other office. This event would be where you invite friends and family who've supported you as you launched this book. Did you hire a sitter to watch your children so you could go write in a quiet spot? Invite her and her friends who might like your book's genre. Invite folks from your church small group or Bible study. For sure, you need your local writing buddies to come enjoy the launch festivities, as they are aware what work and labor you've put into this book baby. More than likely, they've been praying you through the writing, pitching and publishing process—no matter which way you've published.

At the local launch/book signing party you could do some drawings and/or giveaways. Or even read a chapter to the crowd, then allow them to ask you questions about the book, your writing journey or what's next.

For the third option, do both online and in person at the same time. For this, you may need a friend to help with the laptop that the folks online will join on a Zoom Call. During the party time, you can designate a specific time you will go online for a Zoom call with your launch team or others who chose to join in from the Zoom option. Or you could even post this in your Street Team if your Zoom plan can include a larger audience. Make sure you check your Zoom plan to be sure of the amount of Zoom attendees you are permitted to have as plans vary. This would be fantastic if you could project it on a larger screen so the people at the local event could see your team. You could sit down and talk for the Zoom call, or let that friend walk around with you at the party so they can see you mingling with your friends and family.

Or at least be a part of the reading session should you choose to do that. Your friend wouldn't only follow you around, but you would be active in the team's connection and the party. Introduce the team to your spouse and children, your writing friends and critique group, as if they are walking beside you at the event. If you do this though, practice with the person manning the laptop or device you'll use—you want them to walk slow so your Zoom participants don't get seasick from the rapid movement!

Should you decide to do any of the above suggestions, you need to plan and prepare the activities and ask your party helpers prior to the start of the launch session. You'll need to decide if there will be games or drawings and the prizes you will use. You may want to get something like bookmarks printed, so you'll need time for the printer to print. Plus, the time you'll need to design them or hire someone to do that.

If your plan is to have a local launch party, a location will need to be chosen and reserved, which may need to be reserved as soon as you have a release date. Venues book up fast. You may need to ask a friend or family member to help you with refreshments, a cake, etc. No matter which launch day or even launch week party you decide to do, create a plan before you begin the launch session. Make notes ahead of time and do the homework of what you will need and the time to acquire it. When you work ahead on this, not only will the participants of the parties enjoy a great time, so will you.

Chapter 16

End with a Definite Date

It doesn't matter if you will publish with a traditional publisher, go independent, or choose a hybrid option, this remains the same for all. Choose a definite date you will end the work and interaction with a launch team and inform them of the date at the very beginning of the launch team application process.

No one wants to help with a launch and it drags on weeks after the book's launch day. You, the author, will continue to promote your book, but a launch team needs to understand when their job is complete. Keep to that planned date, too.

Not that you won't ask anyone to help continue to promote the book. This is why you've asked the launch team to come over to your street team if they aren't already a part of it.

Once you've launched the book, on occasion you can share a graphic in your street team and ask if anyone would care to *give the book some love* and share the graphic. Some graphics you created can be reused. Change the words on it, or even the background. If one of the graphics says coming soon as the wording, change it to new release, now available or add a quote from the book.

With a definite date, this allows the team to work hard, and not feel taken advantage of. If you've stated the end date on the Launch Team Application, make sure you mark your calendar to remind yourself not to keep going. Your team needs to be informed when the launch is done and you've kept your word on that date. They're more apt to apply next launch for you if you can be counted on to keep your commitment to the team. Is it launch day, the end of launch week, the Friday the week after? This end date will also come into play as you plan what you will do at the end of the launch. Will you plan a Zoom Call after? Will you do a Facebook Live and announce a Grand Prize winner?

With a definite end date, it doesn't matter if you'll do a live, recorded, or emailed message. Take the time to say thank you and the launch session is complete. I hope you will say more than that, but I believe you get my drift.

As I've managed the teams, I found I needed to release the team from duty by the Friday, the week after the launch at the latest. So, if a launch day is a Tuesday, that has them hang around ten more days at the maximum to help finish getting that last push for reviews, returning the Final Task Checklist if you will do a drawing with those, and a couple more shares of graphics that say now available.

Even ending Wednesday, the week after launch is fine too. Since you were savvy and decided before the launch, it's in the schedule already according to your best date to finish. We all are committed to many things in our life. Make sure you've chosen a date you can be there, too.

If you chose not to do a live send off by Facebook Live or Zoom, send a thank-you to everyone on the team. At the very least, send a thank you email. With the thank you, inform them the launch session is complete and you are closing down the launch group. Unless, of course, you've decided to change it to a street team. You should also place a farewell/thank you post in the Facebook Group, then give a week before you close it down to allow all to see your post. Pin it to the top so they will see it.

Bottom line, thank them, and bid them adieu.

Chapter 17

Send All Promised Gifts

ONE WAY TO stay on top of the drawing winners or thank-you gifts is to keep a list of only those specific items. If you do drawings, add the person's name on the list and include a column that says item sent to check off. Keep it handy and make sure you follow through with sending them as soon as possible after the names were drawn. If you held any drawings during the launch session, after launch day is the time to get that list back out and make sure you sent the appropriate prize to everyone who's won. In addition, if you held an online or live event and you did any type of games in which you had winners, make sure those items have been sent as well.

Back when organizing the launch, did you create a thank-you bookmark or some other SWAG for the team? Make sure you send those out within the week after your launch session ends. I suggest to the authors I coach, as soon as you've reached week two or three in the launch session, sit and address the envelopes for a thank-you card or one to accommodate a bookmark. Then your envelopes are ready for you to write a note, stuff and send off after launch day.

The further you move away from the hype of launch week, you will move on to the next book and work on preparations for the launch of that book. You may think about it and try to remember to get the items mailed, but inch by inch, you'll move further away from that thought as time rolls forward on the calendar.

Oh, and life will happen.

While you tidy up your office the week after launch day, put away all things for this current book you've had on the surfaces of your desk. Now is the time to send your thank-you notes, bookmarks, prizes, or any items you've created or purchased for this book launch you haven't sent yet. You don't want to forget. I've seen it happen. Well intentions, busy life and several months down the road, the author has run across a box of items which were supposed to be sent. Yet, life happened, and a day turned into a week, turned into a month, and so on.

Do yourself the favor, clean out your office piles related to this current book, mail off what's needed, pack up everything left over and make room to prepare for the next one.

Chapter 18

Send a Launch Team Survey

At the end of each launch, I send out a Final Task Check-In created in Google Forms. I set it up much like the one I did for the Launch Team Application. This is a great tool if you are going to do a grand prize drawing the week after launch day.

Another free option to use for forms is jotform.-com. I've not used this app as a creator, but I've received forms from others using this company. It seemed easy to use.

I use this survey for the grand prize drawing at the end of the launch session. Those who fill out the form and submit, are included in the drawing. It's your choice how you choose the winner—random name drawn or person with the most checks or answers, or even let them fill in a raffle app like King Sumo or one you prefer. If you go with the most completed tasks, be prepared for ties. Several of my repeat launch team members are hyper goal-driven and will fill that bad boy up with completed task check marks early in the launch session. Not even lying. And oh yes, I love them on the teams I manage. They do the work they've said they would do. Plus, more than what's on the list.

Another option is to use this for your personal information for the next launch. Once information is collected and the deadline has passed, you can turn this form into a spreadsheet so you can see at a glance who did work for the book or not, especially if you've chosen not to keep a Team Task Checklist as described in Chapter Nine. Or, if you did keep the Task Check-list, you can compare the survey to the spreadsheet you've kept up with for the tasks you asked them to do throughout the launch.

The questions you could ask are varied. You need to decide what you're looking for and for what purpose.

Some questions I ask on my Final Task List Check-In:

1. Full name. Google Forms collected the emails, but sometimes email is not a great indicator of who the person is—doggirl248 doesn't tell me who the actual person is.

2. Create a check box list (this is an option in each box section) asking the specifics of which retailers they've posted a review. Some of those are: Amazon, Barnes & Noble, Christian Book, Books A Million,

BookBub, Goodreads, Target, Library Thing, and Kobo.

3. What is your Amazon username? This allows you to check for their posted review if you want to be sure. Again, people don't always use their full name as their username in this case.

4. Copy and paste your Amazon review. I choose the "Long Answer Box" here to allow them room to share that. If it hasn't posted, they can still click on leave a review and it will take them to their review and tell them they've already posted a review. They can then copy and paste their submitted review from that review box back onto their survey form

5. Did you share about the book at least three times during the Launch Week?

6. Did you share the preorder graphic? This applies only if you gave them a preorder graphic.

7. Did you recommend the book to your library?

8. Was I clear in my instructions and expectations for the team?

9. Did I provide you with graphics and tasks? Or was it too much?

10. What else would you like me to tell me you did for the book during the launch session?

11. Would you like to be informed about the next launch?

Whether you decide to use this form or not is up to you. The questions and purpose you use it for is a personal choice. For me, it has saved me a lot of time scrolling through the various sites to look for reviews or if the people posted graphics. At least with this list, I can check activity of the team member should I choose to. With the addition of the actual name/username they've posted under has been a tremendous timesaver, that's for sure.

Chapter 19

Do a Launch Team Recap

IF THIS WAS your first launch, it's imperative to take the time to do a recap of the entire launch of your book as soon as you finish the launch. The good items you did and the ones you feel you should do better or different will still be fresh in your mind. This is a great time to assess this, so you can prepare now what you'll do on your next launch. Or even what you will not do again.

In your recap, include what you've done for the year prior to the actual launch date, not just the launch team session leading up to launch day. Some of those items or activities could include:

1. Did I schedule podcasts, book signings, and meet the author events far enough in advance to give myself the proper time to advertise the event?

2. Was the time I planned for the launch session to allow the team a fair time to assist me in the book's promotion enough to accomplish all I planned?

3. Were the SWAG/thank-you gifts, gifts for drawings, ordered early enough so I had time to get them ready to send right after the launch session?

4. Did I get the book, whether PDF or paperback, to the team at the start of the launch session to allow them enough time to read and promote the book?

5. Was my interaction with my team good—not too little and not too much—and did I remain engaged with the team?

6. Were all promised items out within two weeks after the launch date? For any that still needed to be mailed at the end of the launch, why didn't they go out and how do I fix that next time?

7. What will I do different on my next launch?

8. Will I handle my next launch team any different?

9. Would I change my time frame for the prep needed to accomplish a successful launch?

To do this for yourself will set you up for a better launch the next time around. You will find each launch you do will differ from the one before. Time changes, apps will get better, or you'll find a better way to connect with your team. Be open to those new options that come along. That popular cliché will be your friend—work smarter, not harder.

No matter the assessment you make of what worked or what didn't work, you must look at positives and determine to change the negatives on the next launch. Whether this was your first launch, your first launch with some helpful tips, or even your tenth launch, I promise you—no two launches will be the same.

The people on the team may be all new, half are new, or the same team. Maybe they were super workers on the last launch, but the timing was off for them on this one. It's okay. Give it your best shot and never sit back and not try new things for the launch. Certain items are best left as they are, while new ideas, social media functions and more may change. Be willing to go with what needs to happen on the current lunch.

What I do not want you to do is to take this recap as a reason to beat yourself up or take the attitude of failure. Learn from it. Change what needs changed. Then move on with excitement to the next launch.

Above all else, give yourself grace. You're worth it.

Chapter 20

The Year of the Launch

You've SENT off your manuscript to the publisher if you're on the traditional publication route. If Independent, you've finished the book and off to the editor before you upload to Amazon. Because publishing a book takes time after it leaves your hands to wherever they will make it into a book, there are items and events you can do in the waiting to educate and equip yourself for a better launch session.

Early in the launch year is when you should check on locations for a launch party or for book signings. Most venues or bookstores schedule pretty far out on the calendar, so check early. If you will give out SWAG of any kind, now is the time to decide on what gift items you want to give and get them ordered so they are here on time and ready when you will need them. This is super important if you choose an item which needs engraved or personalized with your book details on them.

These are not items I offer in my Launch Team Management, but I'm aware of the benefits to plan for these events within the year of the launch of your book. While the list below is not a complete list, what follows are a few that came to mind I'd like to share with you.

Join a Launch Team or a Couple.

A great way to see what other launch members could do for you on your launch team is to apply to participate on other authors' launch teams in your genre. And by participate, I mean that in the full sense of the word. Don't be a lurker in the group, scoping out ideas. Remember, you're going to be in the same shoes as that author in a quick minute. You don't want people to join your launch team and only observe what happens in a team. Be the type of launch team member you'd like on your own team—one who is active and enthusiastic.

If chosen for a team, do all the tasks the author asks of you. Take part in the activity to feel the time commitment of the task the author has asked to be done. Make notes of what they did that you liked or found the teammates doing with enthusiasm. It's good to see what it feels like when an author asks you to do too much or too little. Notice if that's the vibe you feel while there.

Whatever you do—don't join and not participate. Never join a bunch of teams and stalk them to see what they do without your own participation.

I've had team members apply to join a launch, then find out they were only there to take notes as they were in the beginning phases of building their own launch team management business. I've learned to spot them. But as an author on your own, you may catch who is on your team but not active, but you may not realize they are only there to take notes. Whatever you do though, please don't be that kind of team member that joins a team to take notes for your own launch or to start a launch business.

During the other author's launch, follow them on their social media sites, GoodReads, Bookbub, and Amazon. Go to their website and subscribe to their newsletter.

At the end of the launch, reach out to the author and tell them you joined to help with the success of their launch. Encourage them and share what you enjoyed about the team. Ask them if they would share a graphic or two for your book launch in the future, or even join your launch team when your launch session comes. Give them the date, if possible, and ask if they would give you honest feedback as this is your first launch—if it is. Tell them you followed them on their social sites and signed up for their newsletter and ask if they would also do so for you. Encourage them and tell them you will cheer for their success. Some may. Some may not. But you will never know unless you ask.

Build Your Social Media as You Wait

Grow your engagement on your own social media sites. Engage! Set up an actionable plan to drop posts into your social media sites several times a week at minimum. Let's say you post on your sites on Monday,

Wednesday, and Friday. On Tuesday, Thursday, and Saturday check the posts you've left and like (or love is my preference) comments that were left by readers. Could the comment someone has left use a reply or a fun emoji in return? Now's the time to do that. You don't need to sit on social media all day and evening seven days a week, but reply within twenty-four hours if possible. This shows your readers you appreciate the time they took to comment. They will want to do more, and new followers will see that you are present on your sites.

As you grow more comfortable in this new schedule of content, try to add a little more or a new social media site you believe your readers may hang out. Authors often ask me if they should be active on all the social media sites so people will find them everywhere. I laugh. Then I ask, "Are you aware of the general audience for each of the social media platforms?

The usual reply I expect follows. "Well, no."

"Tell me your genre and what age category do you think your readers might be?"

"I write historical romance and any age could read my books."

"Yes, they could. But let's be realistic. Who might be more of your typical reader for that?"

"I guess 40-to-70-year-olds?"

"Fair enough. Would that age group be on Snapchat?"

"On snap-what?"

"My point. You aren't familiar with Snapchat. Your reader may not be on Snapchat, MeWe, Clubhouse, Blue Sky, MightyNetworks, WhatsApp or Discord either. Trust me, there are probably more than what I just rattled off that I'm unaware of. Do your homework, find out where your ideal readers are hanging out and make that a place you regularly engage."

Their eyes have glossed over by now and their expression has gone flat. My point for you as an author and one whom will launch their own book, is to not try so hard to be everywhere on every social media site that you ignore the sites your loyal readers will be. Will there be readers of various ages on those other sites? Sure. But, might I remind you—as if you need reminded—we're only given so many minutes and hours in each day, figure out who is your reader and be where they are. Your brain will love you for not overloading it. Not that I've tried to do that or anything like that.

Follow other authors in your genre on their social media sites.

If you aren't already doing this, now is a great time to start. Reach out to some you've read their books. Follow them on their social media sites, sign up for their newsletters, and like and/or comment on their posts now and then. This helps to build the connection to the other writers in your genre. From time to time, reach out and send a private message or email to them through their contact me section of their website. If you've signed up for their newsletter, you could also reply to the newsletter. Share a word of encouragement about their website, posts, or newsletter. If you've read one of their books and liked it, tell them you enjoyed it. Most people appreciate a note of kind words, and I'm sure most authors enjoy a note from another author who is one of their cheerleaders. After all, authors appreciate the work it takes to be an author and enjoy the camaraderie from someone who knows the trials of the writer's journey.

Secure Interviews, Book Signings and More

If you desire to be interviewed for websites/blogs or on Podcasts, make sure you secure them early in the launch year. They make schedules well in advance for most of those and you want the time to research the best fit of sites for you and your book. Secure book signing locations if you will do those. Leave time to find a venue for a launch party if you choose to do one. The size of the party may determine how early you need to reserve the place. Be mindful of what you'd like to do and make the calls to learn the price to rent, if you can bring your own food or they require you to buy from them and the dates available.

Utilize Your Newsletter

This period of waiting for the finished book is the perfect time to build your newsletter subscriber list. The more you build this list, the better chance you gain an excellent group of applicants for your Launch Team Application.

During the year leading up to the launch of the book, engage more with your readers. After you've sent the manuscript in, announce in your newsletter that you've just hit the Submit button for your manuscript and it's off to the publisher. Let subscribers join in with your excitement. To ask for prayer from your readers is a great way to include them on your journey. Don't forget to keep them posted with updates as well. They will become invested and follow along to see when the book will release.

Nine months out, make a consorted effort to push for newsletter subscribers. Give them the information about how you will send the Application for the Launch Team to the newsletter subscribers first, if that's what you choose to do. If your subscriber list is large, you may only send out the application through your newsletter. One of my repeat authors only uses their newsletter people. They feel the newsletter subscribers are their most faithful fans and they like to give them the opportunity first. If the team isn't complete from that first draw from the newsletters, then they put the link to the application in their social media sites. This does not happen often, but it's a nice option.

Six months out, ask your readers to reply with their favorite Podcasts. See if any of them would fit your book for a place to apply to be on the podcast. Your readers can be a great resource to aid you in those interviews.

Five months out, get the buzz rolling on the book

launch. Start the talk about the book and when it will release in your newsletter once a month. On your social media sites, put another big push for newsletter subscribers with a new lead magnet also on your social media sites. How about a Flash Fiction in your newsletter about a character or two that are in the backstory of your upcoming release. Or even a scene you didn't use.

If you decide to share something you've written, the month before you post the news about a new lead magnet, remember to send it to your current subscribers and tell them they get the piece first because they're already subscribed—no need to resubscribe. This helps to keep people from subscribing again so they can get the new story from you. You don't need so many double subscriptions. If you're on a paid plan, you for sure don't want to pay for those doubles or for it to bump you up to the next subscriber level.

Four months out, tell your subscribers a bit about the background to the story. Where did the idea come from? How long did it take you to write this book? Do you have funny stories about the story itself or in your process in writing this book? Start a conversation about the book without spoilers, of course. Let them into your story a little.

Three months out, if you are doing any events for the launch, make a list and share with your subscribers. At this point, you won't have your team chosen, but you can inform your subscribers the dates for any of your events, so they can plan to join you at an event.

You may be shocked where your readers and followers are from, and there may be some close enough to join you.

In the middle of this third month from launch, send out a newsletter with only the Launch Team Application Google Doc link. Give them details about the launch, the book info, the submission deadline and when the team chosen will hear from you. Give yourself and the people the time to respond and you the time to sort through the applications. Use the newsletter and your social media sites if your number of subscribers is small. You can also add a preorder buy link and blurb from the back cover in this month's newsletter if you have one.

Two months out, your team should be chosen, Facebook Group created and they are in the group to get started. In this month's newsletter, put your book and a small blurb about it at the bottom of the newsletter and don't forget that preorder buy link again if you are using.

One month out, your launch team and the tasks and graphics to share are in motion. In your newsletter, put the book and preorder link in your newsletter again. Share a shorter blurb about the book. It could even be your pitch for the book, your initial premise, or the what if that set up the story you wrote.

The options to do for a launch are as varied as the authors or launch team members themselves. Research other ideas to do during that year moving toward the launch day. Find what will work for you. Do the homework and make the plans to do those events or activities to get the news out about your book. Be reasonable.

It might be impossible to hold a beach book signing if you live in the center of the country. Unless you want to spend that much money or time, then go for it. What sounded great a year out may be a bigger financial drain than you ever thought. As you get closer to launch day, the costs will continue to increase. Launch party, prizes, thank-you gifts—they'll all need to be paid. Be wise and stay within your budget.

You'll be glad you did.

Chapter 21

My Final Thoughts on Book Launches

WHILE I HAPPEN to love everything about book launches, I'm aware many become ill or panic at the mention of the term. Maybe that's you. What I hope you got out of this book is my confidence in your ability to have a successful launch session.

My desire was to educate you on the various options of how to manage a team. Also, to equip you with some of my tried-and-true experiences that led to great team accomplishments.

Finally, to encourage you to give it a try. I believe anyone can have a productive and successful launch with enough of the correct tools to get the job done. I've given it my best to give you those tools. May you have a great launch session.

Now, go Launch That Book!

Acknowledgments

Most people think writers sit alone in a room hunched over their keyboards. They type away until they type *the end*, then send it off to a publisher. If only it were that simple. To say it takes a village to write a book, would not be a misuse of that cliché. To write a book is not a one-man or one-woman endeavor. With that, I have a few I'd like to thank here.

A huge thank you to my book endorsers. I hope you realize how much I've appreciated your wisdom and guidance as I have traveled this writing journey to this specific spot. Your encouragement, correction, and graciousness shown when I asked questions, I will always be grateful for. I'm blessed to have been able to sit at your feet to learn.

My daily writer accountability group—SBP—you girls are the bomb-diggity. Mandy Boerma and Sara Turn-quist—so grateful for you. Your prayers, suggestions, cheers, and some moments spent talking me off the ledge were appreciated more than you know.

My Tuesday crew who prayed for me to keep going. Marilyn Nutter, Andrea Merrell, and Lee Russ—I felt those prayers and your encouragement as well. Your excitement when I texted, *all done*, was uplifting. Thank you.

Larry Leech II - Your kind nudge. Your continued encouragement. Your "in my face—spot on" call out when oh so necessary. Your promotion of my book to your clients. Thank you doesn't seem enough. I am grateful for your wisdom and friendship.

My long-time dear friend and dedicated encourager, Katie Kuehl, thank you. Your prayers for me and my writing were greatly appreciated. The many times of reminding me I was born to write and called to follow through with it did not go unheard.

To the biggest cheerleader anyone could have. To the one who daily asked if I did any writing on my books. To the one who wants to see me walk in my calling. Larry, my husband, thank you for the encouragement, brainstorm time, and allowing me to talk through some of the plans for this book the first time I wrote it, and now as this second edition is published. I love you.

Most importantly, thank you Lord for answering that question on June 19, 2011, when I asked what you wanted me to do for you with my life now in a new season. You flipped my Bible to the concordance and the word – WRITE – popped out clear for me to see. Thank you for your unconditional love for and patience with me.

Meet the Author

Tammy Karasek uses humor and wit to bring joy and hope to every aspect in life. Her past, filled with bullying and criticism from family, drives her passion to encourage and inspire others and show them *The Reason* to smile. She's gone from down and defeated to living a "Tickled Pink" life as she believes there's always a giggle wanting to come out!

A writer of romance—with a splash of sass—her debut book, *Launch That Book*, released in 2023—with this second edition published in November 2025. Her work is published in several compilation books: *Coolinary Moments*—a Divine Moments book, The PAC Method for Writers, and Sustaining Life's Victories. She's also a regular team member for The Write Conversation, Blue Ridge Conference, The Write Editing, and New Mercies Cafe.

Connect with Tammy: tammykarasek.com